The Self-Pay Patient

Affordable Healthcare Choices
in the
Age of Obamacare

Sean Parnell

Contents

Acknowledgements

A book like *The Self-Pay Patient* doesn't just spring into being. It takes a lot of assistance, support, guidance, and encouragement. The list of people who helped in some way to make this book a reality is a long one, and I can't thank them all here, but a few people stand out who deserve special recognition.

First, my wife, Anne—it seems like in most acknowledgements the author's husband or wife is listed last, almost as an afterthought. That hardly seems right, especially here in light of all the support, encouragement, and love Anne has shown me through this project and our entire marriage. So thank you, and the same for our son, Ryan, who has been a source of inspiration and joy during this time as well.

I've been extremely fortunate to have been able over many years to work, meet, and discuss with some of the leading practitioners, thinkers, and activists in healthcare, learning from them and picking their brains on the subject of how healthcare can be made more affordable. A few that deserve special recognition include surgeon and former congressman Greg Ganske, John Goodman of the National Center for Public Policy Analysis, and Greg Scandlen of Consumers for Health Care Choices, as well as several doctors, including Dr. Robert Berry of the PATMOS Clinic, Dr. Alieta Eck of the Zarephath Health Clinic, and Dr. Vern Cherewatenko of Simple*Care*..

Some of the material in this book I first discovered working at The Heartland Institute and writing for *Health Care News*, and I'm grateful to Heartland President Joe Bast and everybody else there for allowing me to write on these and other topics, especially because that really wasn't what I'd been hired to do! At Heartland I also had the chance to interact with and learn from two great minds on empowering patients as consumers who both passed away far too soon, Conrad Meier and Lee Tooman. Their insights and lessons remain with me today.

Finally, I have to extend my thanks to all of the self-pay patients who have reached out to me with their own stories and advice since I began this project and my blog, www.TheSelfPayPatient.com. Their information, insights, and encouragement has been inspiring and educational, helping to shape many parts of the book and bring to my attention things that I wasn't aware of. This book is theirs as much as mine, and I am grateful for their support.

To my mother,
who always insisted
I think outside the box.

Introduction

On January 1, 2014, tens of millions of Americans become eligible for subsidies to buy health insurance under the Patient Protection and Affordable Care Act of 2010 (more commonly known as Obamacare), and many will be able to buy insurance coverage previously out of reach because of pre-existing medical conditions or high premiums. Millions will take advantage of this opportunity, but at the same time millions will not. The Congressional Budget Office predicts that 30 million Americans will remain uninsured even after Obamacare is fully implemented.

For the young, insurance may seem like a bad deal that asks them to pay inflated prices for insurance that delivers few benefits. Others will find insurance is still unaffordable, and more will simply reject participation in what I call bureaucratic medicine and opt to escape Obamacare and become or remain self-pay patients, who pay directly for most or all of their healthcare.

Tens of millions more Americans will find themselves in high-deductible plans that require them to pay up to $5,000 or more for healthcare out of their own pocket before they begin to receive many benefits.

This book is for Americans who are or will become self-pay patients, and it provides detailed information explaining how by paying cash for most medical services and finding alternative ways of funding and paying for major medical expenses they can get the healthcare services and financial security they need, often at a fraction of the cost of traditional health insurance. As a result of becoming a self-pay patient, they can escape bureaucratic medicine.

What do I mean by the term *bureaucratic medicine*? Simply put, it's the system that most Americans participate in today (or are locked out of) in which healthcare is provided with the heavy involvement of third parties, typically insurers or government programs. These third parties know little about the individual needs and circumstances of each patient and usually have little if any medical training that would allow them to diagnose or treat a patient, but because of their role as the payer of healthcare bills on behalf of an insurer, employer, or government program, their role in determining what healthcare you receive is as big as you and your doctor, maybe even more. And their job usually isn't to make sure you get the care you need, but to save the payer money.

To cite just one example, I know a woman who suffers from severe migraines, so bad that she's had to go to the emergency room several times and has at times had to spend four to five days out of each month in bed, in a dark room, not moving or doing anything else because it would make her migraine even worse.

In the middle of the last decade, it was discovered that Botox, if injected in the right spots in the head, neck, and face, could prevent migraines or at least dramatically reduce their frequency and severity. She was fortunate enough to be part of the clinical trial that proved that Botox could be effective in treating migraines and responded extremely well to the treatment. Even better, she was able to get her employer's health insurance to cover the shots, which ran about $900 and were administered 3 or 4 times a year.

Then she changed jobs, and her new insurance wouldn't cover the Botox injections even though they had been proven to work. A variety of bureaucratic reasons were given: her doctor's office hadn't put the right code on a form, or the doctor's language in her record didn't conform to exactly what the insurer needed it to say for the treatment to be approved. The doctor's billing staff didn't talk with the staffer who handled appeals, so the appeal wasn't submitted on time. More bureaucratic snafus occurred, and each time the insurer said the same thing: we will not pay for this. At one point they misread the doctor's notes as saying that Botox had not been shown to help her when it said exactly the opposite.

Finally, after more than six months; several cycles of terrible migraines, bills for thousands of dollars that she struggled to pay; and hundreds of hours on the part of the patient, her doctor and staff, and insurance bureaucrats, the insurer relented and agreed to cover the Botox—after the patient threatened to file a complaint with the state attorney general.

Several weeks after receiving the approval, another letter was sent from the insurer again denying coverage of the Botox treatment. Fortunately, at this point, a few phone calls cleared the matter up, and she was now able to get the treatment that helps to keep her from suffering from debilitating migraines.

This is bureaucratic medicine, where third-party payers who know little about healthcare or the patient are put in a position where they make what can literally be life-or-death decisions over what medical care will or will not be provided. Instead of medical decisions made by you and your doctor based on what is in your best interest, you are at the mercy of some probably well-intentioned individual sitting in a cubicle hundreds or thousands of miles away whose job it is to see if the right boxes have been checked on the form, the right codes have been entered, and whether the treatment recommended by your doctor matches their menu of approved treatments.

This system doesn't just deny patients the medical care they need;

it causes immense frustration and wastes countless hours of people's time in trying to argue with their insurer or benefits administrator and navigate the system to get the care they need. It is also hugely expensive, driving up the cost of care by requiring doctors, hospitals, insurers, and others to hire huge numbers of billing specialists, claims processors, and others whose job is to do everything but actually deliver healthcare.

It doesn't have to be this way, and for millions of Americans today it isn't. Either because they don't want to be part of bureaucratic medicine or because the high cost of this type of medicine has forced them out of it, or because they have a high deductible insurance plan, these people have found themselves as self-pay patients for most or all of their healthcare. By not buying health insurance or by buying a high-deductible plan that only covers truly catastrophic medical costs, they have escaped bureaucratic interference in healthcare and put healthcare decisions back in the hands of patients and doctors—where it should be.

For many people, the idea of paying directly for their healthcare seems strange, even frightening. Isn't healthcare hugely expensive, after all?

In fact, the healthcare that most people get isn't all that expensive, at least not compared to other expenses people routinely have. When you consider that for most people buying health insurance means paying several hundred or even more than a thousand dollars each month so that the few times each year they visit a doctor they only have to pay a $20 copay instead of a $100 charge for an office visit, it's health insurance that's expensive, not healthcare!

That doesn't mean that insurance doesn't have an important role. If you get diagnosed with a serious disease like cancer or are badly injured in a car accident, or have something else happen to you that causes major medical expenses, you probably want and need insurance or something that functions like insurance.

The good news is that there are plenty of low-cost options for self-pay patients, including certain types of insurance that aren't regulated the same way as conventional health insurance and that will provide money to pay your medical bills if you are diagnosed with a serious illness or are badly injured. There is an entire marketplace of providers including doctors, nurses, hospitals, clinics, drugstores, and online websites that are all aimed at meeting the needs of self-pay patients, often for a lower cost and higher quality than what you can find in the system of bureaucratic medicine.

So whether you like Obamacare but just can't afford to buy insurance even with subsidies or strongly oppose the law and are looking for a way to escape its mandates, or you have insurance but it comes with a high deductible, this book is for you. It may even be for you if you have "good" health insurance with a low deductible and modest copays because there are some treatments and procedures that many insurers still won't cover and you will have to pay out of your pocket for.

The Self-Pay Patient provides specific information on how to find insurers, doctors, hospitals, pharmacies, clinics, laboratories, and other medical providers that cater to self-pay patients who can save hundreds, thousands, or even tens of thousands of dollars a year.

One final note about Obamacare: this book is not about beating up on that law and explaining how terrible it is, or what a more sensible reform might have been, or what should replace it if it is repealed or ultimately fails. There are plenty of books out there that do these things, some of them quite well written and others less so.

But one thing should be clear: Obamacare is built upon and expands the existing system of bureaucratic medicine and for that reason is unlikely to do much if anything to change the waste, frustration, and inflated expenses that define the current system. The information in this book not only provides information that can help almost every American get the healthcare they need, but if embraced by enough people can show the way toward a healthcare system that puts patients and healthcare providers, not bureaucrats, at the center of medicine.

Chapter 1

Explaining Obamacare

While this book is not about The Affordable Care Act (more commonly known as Obamacare, which is what I'll refer to it as for the rest of the book), it's worth taking a little time to understand just how it will operate and how the subsidies, individual and business mandates, and other provisions will affect you.

Most people think that Obamacare requires all Americans to purchase insurance through the exchanges or to get it from employers, with the exception of older Americans enrolled in Medicare or poorer Americans who are covered by Medicaid. This commonly held understanding is wrong. Many Americans are in fact exempt from the Obamacare mandate and the tax that can be levied on the uninsured.

Before we get to those exemptions, here is a brief explanation of how Obamacare will work.

Under Obamacare, Medicaid is available to Americans whose family income is less than 138 percent of the federal poverty level (FPL) in the states that have expanded their programs *if* they are not also eligible to get insurance from their employer. A single person with an income of $15,856 (138 percent of FPL) or less would be eligible for Medicaid, while a family of four with $32,499 or less in income would be eligible.

Employers who have 50 or more full-time employees are required to make insurance available to employees or face a $2,000 fine per employee. Originally intended to go into effect in 2014 at the same time the exchanges open, it has been delayed until 2015 after the Obama administration could not determine how to implement it in time.

For those who are not able to get insurance through Medicaid or their employer, Obamacare requires that they either buy insurance in the individual market (typically through an exchange) or pay a tax for being uninsured unless they qualify for an exemption.

The exchange is simply an online marketplace for people who can't get insurance through their job. Unlike many marketplaces, however, the only product that can be sold on an exchange is government-designed health insurance based on bureaucratic medicine, offered by those insurers that the government thinks you should be allowed to buy from.

Americans who purchase their insurance through the exchange may be eligible to receive subsidies based on their income. The subsidies are structured so that, between 100 percent and 400 percent of FPL, no individual or family has to pay more than a certain percentage of their income in health insurance premiums. The percentage is lower for those with lower incomes compared to those with higher incomes receiving subsidies.

For example, at 100 percent of FPL, no individual or family is expected pay more than 2 percent of their income in insurance premiums. So using 2013 FPL numbers, an individual earning 100 percent of FPL would not have to pay more than $230 for the entire year in premiums, or less than $20 a month. A family of four earning 100 percent would only have to pay about $471, or less than $40 a month.

Individuals and families are expected to pay much more for

their insurance as their income rises. At the highest income where subsidies are provided, individuals and families are expected to pay 9.5 percent of their income. So an individual earning $45,960 (400 percent of FPL) is expected to pay about $4,366 each year towards their insurance, while a family earning $94,200 would pay $8,949 in premiums before subsidies kick in.

Starting at 401 percent of FPL there are no subsidies, and those purchasing insurance are expected to pay the full premium. Those premiums are likely to be very high compared to insurance available before Obamacare's exchanges opened.

Because unsubsidized premiums are going to be high, Congress exempted individuals and families from having to purchase health insurance if the premium would be more than 8 percent of income. Effectively this exempts millions of Americans who earn more than 400 percent of FPL from paying the Obamacare tax if they don't purchase insurance, particularly middle-aged and older Americans who would face higher premiums.

Whether you are exempt will depend on what the lowest-available bronze-level plan for your age is in your state. Once that premium hits 8 percent of your income, the exemption begins. That means an individual earning more than $45,960 will be exempt once a bronze annual premium hits about $3,800, while a family of four earning more than $94,200 will be exempt once the premium reaches approximately $7,550. Other than younger individuals and families under about 35 (depending on state), the unsubsidized premiums are likely to be higher than 8 percent of income for millions of Americans above 400 percent of the poverty level.

A brief review of income data for the American public makes one thing clear: tens of millions of Americans earning middle-class and upper-middle class incomes are free from having to pay Obamacare's penalty for not purchasing insurance.

There are several other exemptions, most of which are very narrowly tailored. For example, incarcerated prisoners (the taxpayer picks up the tab there), members of certain religious faiths (such as the Amish), undocumented immigrants, and Native Americans (who can receive care through Indian Health Services) are exempt. The most interesting exemption, one that tens of millions of Americans may be eligible for, is for members of healthcare-sharing ministries (discussed in the next chapter).

For those who don't buy approved health insurance and don't qualify for an exemption, they may have to pay a tax to the IRS. By 2016, individuals and families will have to pay either $695 per adult (half that for an uninsured child, up to a maximum of $695 for 2 uninsured children) or 2.5 percent of adjusted income.

But there is an important caveat: even though tens of millions of Americans are subject to the tax if they are uninsured, the federal government has very little ability to collect the tax. Unlike nearly every other tax, the IRS is prohibited from seeking civil or criminal penalties for people who refuse to pay the tax, and they are also prohibited from garnishing wages or seizing assets. In fact, the only way the IRS can collect the tax is by reducing your tax refund.

What this means is that people who prefer not to purchase health insurance under Obamacare but who don't qualify for one of the exemptions may not have to pay the fine for being uninsured if they are not owed a tax refund.

This is not a risk-free decision, and people should carefully weigh the decision to avoid paying the tax if they chose to remain uninsured. Among other risks, it is entirely possible that a future Congress will see a large amount of unpaid Obamacare individual mandate taxes and change the law in order to force people to pay them.

Obamacare's first provisions began going into effect in 2010, starting with fairly popular measures like allowing adult children up to age 26 to remain on parents' health insurance policies. Beginning in 2014, however, the exchange, tax credits, and Medicaid expansion go into effect. Early signs indicate the program still faces significant hurdles in technology, public awareness, and "rate shock" for younger Americans who may elect to pay the penalty instead of buying insurance they see little value in.

How or whether Obamacare will work is still anyone's guess and depends heavily on how you define *work*. But there is little doubt at this point that tens of millions of Americans will not want to or will be unable to take advantage of the law's benefits for a wide range of reasons, including unaffordability or an unwillingness to continue to be part of the bureaucratic medical system that Obamacare builds on. Tens of millions of Americans will gain coverage by buying high-deductible insurance that in effect requires them to become self-pay patients for most of their care.

All of this means that, regardless of whether Obamacare lives up to the hopes and expectations of the law's supporters or more closely resembles its critics' worst fears, a substantial number of Americans will be self-pay patients, many for the first time.

Chapter 2

Funding Healthcare without Health Insurance

Health insurance plays a vital role in helping people afford needed medical care. In many ways, people are generally better off with health insurance than without it.

One thing to keep in mind is that there are several alternatives to the health insurance that is offered through Obamacare's exchanges. This chapter details three relatively low-cost alternatives that will allow you and your family to know that in the event of a serious injury or illness, you will have funding to help pay for your needed care. There is also a brief review of several other funding options for healthcare at the end of this chapter.

Paying Cash for Medical Care—Advantages and Disadvantages

Most of the options given here for funding major medical care involve you, the patient, spending cash to get the treatment and care you need. There are some major advantages and a few disadvantages to this. Fortunately, most of the disadvantages can often be dealt with relatively simply and are discussed in later chapters, but here are a few things to keep in mind with being a cash-paying patient:

Pros:

- There are no networks or restricted lists of doctors, hospitals, or labs—you are free to see any medical provider you want.

- There are no pre-approvals to see a specialist.

- There are no insurance or government bureaucrats deciding what is and is not appropriate treatment, only you and your medical provider.

- By paying cash, you can negotiate significant discounts or pay better prices than insurance companies or government programs.

Cons:

- While you may get a better price than insurers and the government, you may not. Many providers are simply not set up to deal with cash-paying patients and instead expect you to pay the inflated price that they then discount for insurers.

- You may wind up owing more for your treatments than you can afford, even after relying on the options given here.

Healthcare-Sharing Ministries

Healthcare-sharing ministries have been around for nearly thirty years, and hundreds of thousands of Americans have had billions of dollars in healthcare expenses paid for by fellow members.

Healthcare-sharing ministries are not insurance, although in many ways they operate the same way. Based on Biblical principles, members join and voluntarily agree to share the medical expenses of fellow members. Each month, members give a fixed amount, typically based on their age and family composition, similar to an insurance premium. Members can select the amount of healthcare costs they are able and willing to pay for themselves before asking fellow members to pay their medical bills, similar to an insurance deductible.

Once an individual or family reaches their threshold, they submit their medical bills to the ministry, which then either sends the needed funds directly to the member or matches them with other members who directly give the money to the member. Requests that members pray for others with healthcare needs is also a common part of the ministries' work.

The costs of joining one of these ministries is generally much less than insurance. A 25-year old individual in normal health willing to be personally responsible for up to $2,500 in health expenses would pay $107 a month through one of the ministries and $110 through another, while a family of four with a 52-year old as its oldest member would pay $482. Insurance policies with similar levels of cost sharing can be twice these amounts or more. This level of savings is fairly typical among the four sharing ministries that currently exist.

While sharing ministries generally cover fewer services than traditional insurance, it can hardly be considered skimpy. Covered medical needs listed by one ministry include cancer treatment, maternity costs, carpal tunnel treatment, diabetes, heart conditions, organ transplants, and injuries that are treated by any doctor or in an emergency room.

Another benefit of sharing ministries, at least for many Americans, is that they are completely exempt from any of the mandates that Obamacare and the states might impose in terms of required benefits, so the controversial requirement that health insurance offer coverage for contraception, sterilization, and possibly even abortion does not apply to sharing ministries. For tens of millions of Americans concerned about their premium dollars being used to fund services they find highly objectionable, sharing ministries offer an excellent way to get their healthcare financing needs met without violating their consciences.

There are some drawbacks and limitations to sharing ministries. As noted, they are not insurance, but voluntary associations based entirely on faith. It does seem to have worked out well for members of these organizations though—to date all four ministries report that they have never failed to pay an eligible need.

In addition, pre-existing conditions may or may not be covered depending on whether a person is currently being treated for one or has been treated in the past, and there may be other limits placed on how much can be shared.

There are also limits on what they will pay for. As organizations that mostly serve practicing Christians, they will not pay for abortion. Mental healthcare and substance abuse can also be seriously limited by the eligibility guidelines, and they typically will not pay for expenses associated with illegal acts, intoxication, or drug abuse. Anyone considering pursuing membership in a healthcare-sharing ministry would be advised to carefully scrutinize the restrictions to make sure they are comfortable with what is and is not eligible to be paid through the ministry.

Three of the four sharing ministries that currently exist require that members be practicing Christians. Depending on the ministry, this may involve getting a pastor to sign a letter attesting that the individual or family attends church regularly and having to sign a statement affirming faith in Christ. Members are also generally expected to conform to relatively conservative teachings on sex, meaning that members agree to confine sex to marriage between a man and a woman.

One organization, Liberty HealthShare, does allow people of any faith (or no faith at all) to join. In most other ways it is similar to the three other ministries.

Undocumented immigrants are welcome in three of the four ministries, meaning that eleven million current residents who may need medical care and funding for that care have an option (Obamacare explicitly excludes these immigrants from getting coverage through the Exchanges or the Medicaid expansion).

There is another key benefit to being a member of a health-care-sharing ministry: Congress specifically exempted members from having to pay the Obamacare tax penalty for being uninsured! Because ministries are not insurance but their members do have an alternative method of paying for their medical care, Congress included language in Obamacare saying that members of health-care-sharing ministries are exempt from the tax penalty.

Unfortunately, the cost of getting this exemption was Congress limiting the exemption to members of currently existing ministries (the ministries did not ask for this, or so I've been told) in order to prevent other faiths from establishing similar sharing ministries. This decision makes Liberty HealthShare the only option for non-Christians who are interested in the sharing ministry approach.

For tens of millions of Americans who are looking for an alternative to Obamacare (or are not allowed to get coverage through it, like undocumented immigrants), healthcare-sharing ministries provide a relatively inexpensive way to ensure that they have the money to pay for needed healthcare.

List of Healthcare-Sharing Ministries with Contact Information
• Samaritan Ministries, www.samaritanministries.org, info@samaritanministries.org, (888) 268-4377
• Christian Care Ministry, www.mychristiancare.org, info@mychristiancare.org, (800) 772-5623
• Christian Healthcare Ministries, www.chministries.org, (800) 791-6225
• Liberty HealthShare, www.libertyhealthshare.org/, (855) 585-5237

Critical Illness, Fixed Benefit, and Accident Insurance Policies

Another option is what is known as critical illness, accident, and fixed benefit insurance. These are three similar types of policies that provide a cash payout when an insured is diagnosed with a specific illness or injury such as cancer, stroke, or a heart attack. And for many Americans, that's all they want: something that will protect them from a major, catastrophic medical expense.

The average cost of treating cancer is nearly $38,000, while treatment for a heart condition averages about $29,000, according to government research. Having to pay out-of-pocket for these treatments could bankrupt many families, or at least impose a huge financial burden on them.

With a critical illness policy, however, you can get a benefit anywhere from $5,000 to $1 million upon diagnosis of either of these conditions, giving you the cash you need to get treatment. Not only that, but it can also be used to pay for missed income or to pay for a nurse or someone to help around the house while you are recovering.

The cost of critical illness policies is significantly less than Obamacare's health insurance policies. According to the website of the American Association of Critical Illness Insurance Policies, a 40-year-old, nonsmoking male would pay around $1,200 a year for a policy that would give him $50,000 cash in the event he was diagnosed with cancer or had a heart attack.

Smaller and larger policy amounts are available as well, and prices vary based on age and the size of the payout as well as your health.

Similar to critical illness insurance is accident insurance. These policies pay a fixed amount for injuries that result in a trip to see the doctor, or to the emergency room, or that require hospitalization. One fairly typical policy offered by one insurer pays $1,000 for hospital admission and $400 for a trip to the emergency room, while another offers up to $5,000 for a broken arm and $300 per night spent in the hospital.

While critical illness policies can cover all of the cost of treating a major illness, accident insurance policies tend to be less generous. The amounts provided typically only cover a fraction of the cost of the treatment. For example, an emergency room visit can average between $600 and $1,350, far more than a $400 benefit.

But a $400 benefit is certainly better than a $0 benefit, which is what Obamacare offers to anyone who doesn't sign up for expensive comprehensive insurance. The rates are extremely reasonable, typically between $20 and $50 month depending on insurer and benefit levels, and unlike both critical illness and health insurance, the rates don't vary much by age.

A variant of accident insurance is fixed-benefit insurance. These tend to offer more generous benefits and can also include cash payments to pay for routine visits to a doctor's office and even inpatient and outpatient surgery. Because of the more generous benefits they are more expensive than accident insurance, although still far more affordable than an Obamacare insurance policy. One major national insurer offers a fixed-benefit insurance plan starting at $67 a month for an individual and $134 for a family.

You probably will recognize many of the insurance companies that offer these policies. AFLAC, Aetna, Mutual of Omaha, and Cigna are among the dozens of insurance companies offering critical illness and accident insurance.

The bad news is that these policies aren't necessarily available to everyone. Many employers offer critical illness and accident insurance to their employees, and some insurance companies will accept applicants who want to purchase these policies on their own. But some insurers only work through employers, limiting the availability of this insurance.

In addition, these insurance policies are underwritten and can exclude pre-existing conditions. So if you've been diagnosed with cancer already or have had a heart attack in the past, you may not qualify for these insurance policies, particularly critical illness insurance.

For people who can obtain critical illness and accident insurance policies, they can provide the needed funding for the major medical expenses that most of us are concerned about like cancer or a heart attack for a fraction of the cost of traditional health insurance. A 40-year-old pairing a $50,000 critical illness policy with a more generous accident insurance policy might pay only $1,800 a year, compared to double or triple that amount for health insurance. In many ways they would have coverage comparable to health insurance, particularly once deductibles, copays, and-co-insurance are figured into the calculation.

Select List of Critical Illness and Accident Insurance Companies

For individuals

- Mutual of Omaha, www.mutualofomaha.com/critical-illness-insurance, (800) 606-4371

- Assurant Health, www.assuranthealth.com/corp/ah/HealthPlans/critical-illness-insurance.htm and www.assuranthealth.com/corp/ah/HealthPlans/Fixed-Benefit-Insurance-Plan-Details.htm, (800) 647-9106

- AFLAC, www.aflac.com/individuals/policies.aspx, (800) 992-3522

- Golden Rule, www.goldenrule.com/critical-illness/, (800) 273-8082 and www.goldenrule.com/accident-plus-benefit/, (800) 944-4699

- Humana, www.humana-one.com/supplemental-insurance/critical-illness/ and www.humana-one.com/supplemental-insurance/supplementalaccident/default.asp, (877) 237-4192

- American Fidelity Assurance Company, www.afadvantage.com/for-individuals/insurance-plans.aspx, (800) 654-8489

For employers

- MetLife, www.metlife.com/individual/employee-benefits/index.html?WT.ac=GN_individual_employee-benefits, (800) 638-5433

- Principal Financial Group, www.principal.com/grouplh/critical-illness.htm, (800) 986-3343

You may also find critical illness and accident insurance coverage available from these and other insurers at www.ehealthinsurance.com/accident-insurance/find-coverage/ and www.ehealth-insurance.com/critical-illness-insurance, or find an insurance broker who can help you at the National Association of Health Underwriters www.nahu.org/consumer/findagent2.cfm

Short-term Health Insurance

Another option for people who can't afford or don't see value in Obamacare's high-priced health insurance plans are what are known as either short-term or limited-duration health insurance. These policies, offered by major insurers, have been around for decades and in the past have served college students, the unemployed, newly-employed persons waiting for employer-sponsored coverage to begin, and other people expecting to need health insurance for a relatively short period before moving on to another long-term plan.

These policies have a duration of less than one year and can have a term as short as a few months or even one month. They can typically be renewed year after year, although limitations on pre-existing conditions can apply, and you can be turned down for coverage or be charged a higher rate if you are in poor health.

Aside from the shorter duration of these policies, in most ways they work just like insurance available before Obamacare. Policies feature a wide range of deductibles, copays, and co-insurance, and provide coverage of healthcare needs comparable to pre-Obamacare policies (pregnancy-related costs are typically excluded though). Many policies have networks of doctors where you will receive the discounted provider network rate.

Because they are exempt from the Obamacare regulations, they are generally much less expensive than the policies that can be bought through the exchange or from an employer. Depending on the state you live in, an individual policy for a 42-year-old male can be as little as $55 a month and a family policy approximately $200 a month with a $5,000 deductible and 20 percent co-insurance.

For an individual or family that would like to keep something resembling pre-Obamacare insurance, a short-term or limited-duration insurance policy may be the perfect solution.

Companies Selling Short-term Health Insurance
• HCC Medical Insurance Services, www.hccmis.com/, (866) 400-7106
• Golden Rule Insurance, www.goldenrule.com/short-term-health-insurance/, (800) 273-8113
• Assurant Health, www.assuranthealth.com/corp/ah/HealthPlans/short-term-health-insurance.htm, (800) 647-9106
• Aetna, http://healthinsurance.aetna.com/health-plans/short-term-temporary, (800) 217-2386
• Humana, www.humana-one.com/health-insurance-news/short-term-medical-health-insurance-product-launch.aspx, (866) 215-6839
• You may also find short-term health insurance options at www.ehealthinsurance.com/short-term-health-insurance/find-coverage/

Other Healthcare Financing Options

The three previously described ways of financing healthcare are, or function as, insurance—less comprehensive in some ways, different, and a little unorthodox, but they all basically work on the same basis, where you put in a little money (relatively speaking) each month and in the event of a major medical illness or injury, you get the funding needed to pay for some, most, or all of your care.

But if you elect not to join a healthcare sharing ministry or purchase one of the insurance products described above, you are still likely to have some medical needs that will need to be paid for. In most cases, it will be relatively inexpensive healthcare costs, like an annual physical or a trip to an urgent-care center for a sprained ankle, while in other cases it will be for more expensive care such as the birth of a child or a broken arm. It may even be a truly catastrophic medical need with a matching pricetag, like a heart attack or treatment for cancer.

Ideally, you're wealthy enough to pay for these things out of your own pocket. For most people, though, medical expenses like the birth of a child or cancer treatment would be major financial burdens without some form of insurance or insurance-like financing. Here are a few additional recommendations on how to pay for these expenses, whether you have some form or insurance or insurance-like financing or are footing the entire bill yourself for you medical care:

- Medical bills related to vehicle accidents can easily be tens of thousands of dollars, which can be paid for with relatively inexpensive personal injury or medical payments coverage as part of your automobile insurance. Consider choosing a high benefit level, $25,000 or more.

- Many healthcare expenses are fairly low-cost. You can just pay these out of pocket from the same source as you pay for your groceries, new tires, clothes, travel, and other living expenses (the following chapters will tell you how to get the best prices for your healthcare).

- If possible, try to have sufficient funds in a health savings account or other savings account that can fund an unexpected medical need that is beyond your ability to pay out of pocket.

- You can always pay for healthcare with a credit card as well. It's not ideal, but it will allow you to get the healthcare you need in a timely fashion. Consider getting a credit card with a relatively high limit and putting that away with the intent of using it only in the event of a truly expensive medical need.

- There are lenders who specialize in loans for medical treatment purposes. Much of their business focuses on procedures that aren't typically covered by any insurer, such as cosmetic surgery and bariatric surgery, but they do also fund more necessary treatments and can offer rates that are typically lower than many credit cards.

- In the event of a truly catastrophic medical bill, you may have to consider accessing retirement accounts or getting a home equity loan, or otherwise dipping into your savings. In some instances penalties are waived for early withdrawals from retirement accounts to pay for medical care, and the interest rates on home equity loans are generally much less than a credit card (and it's tax deductible, too).

- Consider joining a concierge or direct care practice, which essentially offers prepaid healthcare services from primary-care doctors at a relatively low cost (you'll learn more about these in the next chapter).

- In the event you are diagnosed with cancer or have a heart attack or some other serious illness or injury and don't have the ability to pay for your past and future care, you may want to consider purchasing an Obamacare insurance policy through an exchange. You can't be turned down, and you won't be charged a higher premium because of your medical history.

Not all of these options are ideal or practical for everyone. The important thing to remember is that your health is vital, and you should be prepared and willing to spend whatever funds you need to in order to preserve or regain it!

Obamacare as a Safety Net:
Is It Cheating or Gaming the System?

Healthcare-sharing ministries, critical illness and accident insurance, and temporary insurance are excellent options for people who can't afford, don't see value in, or object to the comprehensive health insurance policies that Obamacare tries to steer most Americans into. For the large majority of people, these options will be more than satisfactory in meeting their medical funding needs.

A small number of people may find after several years or decades, however, that their medical funding needs can no longer be met by these options. They may hit the maximum amount that a healthcare-sharing ministry can fund, or their treatment for an illness or injury might exceed by a significant amount their benefit from a critical illness or accident policy, or they may not be able to renew a temporary insurance policy.

If you are one of the few that this happens to, or you are concerned about this happening to you, there is a safety net: Obamacare. Because the law prohibits insurers from denying applicants based on health status or pre-existing conditions, no matter your medical history you will be able to buy insurance at standard rates for your age, and because you are likely to have saved tens of thousands or even hundreds of thousands of dollars over the years by not paying premiums for high-priced health insurance, it may be more affordable for you to purchase health insurance through an Obamacare exchange if the options described here somehow don't pan out.

Some may say this is gaming the system, taking advantage of loopholes by not having bought insurance before getting seriously ill or injured, and that doing the things described in this chapter amounts to shirking your personal responsibility. I strongly disagree.

By arranging alternate, private non-Obamacare financing for your healthcare in the first place, you have in fact taken personal responsibility and even saved the taxpayers money in the process. Critics of the approach described here would give you only two choices: buy high-priced, comprehensive insurance that you may not be able to afford or see value in, or go completely uninsured and rely entirely on government-funded care for the indigent. They would leave an uninsured person (by traditional measures) completely vulnerable to financial devastation in the event of a serious illness or injury without any ability to pay for medical care other than relying on taxpayers to pick up the full tab.

This book describes a third possibility, one that can ensure that even though you are uninsured, you are still able to fund and pay for your needed care and won't impose a burden on taxpayers or providers, and that is, in my opinion, a far more responsible way to handle things than simply telling people who can't afford insurance to buy insurance.

Chapter 3

Primary Care for Routine Health Needs

Primary care accounts for nearly 90 percent of healthcare services in America today (but a much smaller share of overall costs), and generally speaking this is inexpensive care that many people can afford to pay for out of pocket. But because bureaucratic medicine caters to insurance companies and government payers, self-pay patients can face challenges in getting the best deals and value for their healthcare dollars. Bureaucratic medicine is set up so that patients typically only have to pay a small copay for both minor and major medical expenses, or the patient's share of the bill can't be determined at the time of service until an insurer has reviewed the bill and determined what the allowable charge is or what the negotiated discount is.

As a result, your doctor's office may be completely bewildered when you ask what the price of an office visit is or how much it will cost to get a simple injury treated. Most doctors don't even know what they charge for simple procedures or visits because they just take whatever reimbursement the big insurance companies say they will pay. Trying to get a real price from a doctor's office in advance of your visit can be a frustrating experience.

Fortunately this is changing. Thousands of doctors have been bailing out of bureaucratic medicine and setting up cash-only, concierge, or direct-care practices that are built around self-pay patients and keeping insurance and government bureaucrats out of the exam room. These are most often primary-care physicians like general practitioners, family practice doctors, and internists, but some specialists are cash-only or at least cash-friendly as well.

In addition, thousands of what are known as convenient care or retail healthcare clinics have been opened around the country, often in retail locations like drugstores, and they typically post their real prices for all to see.

Several entrepreneurs have also stepped up and have developed online websites that cater to self-pay patients, and there are other options as well that help ensure that you are able to get the best price possible for your medical care as a self-pay patient.

Cash-only and Cash-friendly Practices

A growing number of doctors have decided to eliminate insurers from their practices and simply post their prices and ask that their patients pay them just like any other service provider such as a mechanic or accountant. In doing so they are typically able to offer much lower prices to patients than the insurer-paid, bureaucratic medical model.

One doctor who runs a cash-only practice in Tennessee describes his practice this way:

> *PATMOS EmergiClinic does not accept any third-party payment and makes no apologies for this. In order to keep costs down for the uninsured and the increasing number of patients who have high copays and deductibles, we choose not to assume the massive overhead involved in billing third-party payers. This has the added benefit of eliminating bureaucratic hassles and*

intrusions into the doctor-patient relationship, ensuring strict confidentiality of patient information, and keeping our typical charges usually between the cost of an oil change and a brake job.

His website lists prices for several visit types and procedures, including a 15-minute scheduled appointment for $60, treatment of a complex cut of less than one inch for $135, and earwax removal for $30 (one ear) or $45 (both ears).

There are literally thousands of doctors who have abandoned bureaucratic medicine and embraced cash-only practices or at least made their prices transparent and give self-pay patients the best prices because they don't have to deal with insurance reimbursements. One doctor in Austin, Texas, charges $30 for primary care visits for a single medical issue, $40 for 2 or more medical issues. That's less than many copays paid by those with comprehensive insurance!

One of the chief benefits for both doctors and patients is that there is no insurance or government bureaucrat trying to tell them how to practice medicine and what is 'covered' and what isn't. Doctors also can spend more time with patients learning about them, allowing them to better treat their patients.

There are several sources to find cash-only or cash-friendly doctors. If you can't find one near you from these sources, consider calling your current doctor or doctors in your area and asking if they provide a discount for prompt, full payment in cash.

Finding a Cash-Only or Cash-Friendly Doctor

Here are several online sources for finding doctors that are specifically geared towards cash-paying patients.

- SimpleCare is an association of patients and medical providers and includes listings of doctors who commit to giving cash-paying patients their best price, searchable here: http://simplecare.com/about-patients.asp.

- Association of American Physicians and Surgeons, a society of physicians who support the practice of private medicine, they have compiled a list of cash-only and cash-friendly practices available here: https://aaps.wufoo.com/reports/m5p6z0/.

- PricePain.com, online search tool for doctors offering cash prices: www.pricepain.com/.

- DocCost.com, similar to PricePain.com: www.doccost.com/.

You can also do a Google search for the terms direct pay or cash only and doctor and the name of the state you live in. Often you will find news coverage of these practices that can allow you to find one near you. If you currently have a doctor, consider talking with them directly about becoming a cash-friendly practice. Explain to them that you will pay in full promptly at the time of service, without any delay or insurance claims to file, and you want to know you won't have to pay inflated charges that are much higher than what insurers pay.

Concierge and Direct-Care Practices

Another option that might be valuable for some self-pay patients, particularly those that expect to need medical attention more than a few times a year (especially important for families with newborns and young children, or those with a manageable chronic condition) are what are known as concierge and direct-care medical practices. These practices are ideal ways to ensure affordable and typically quick access to high-quality primary care.

In concierge medicine, a doctor is paid a retainer (usually monthly, sometimes annually or semi-annually) by the patient. This retainer can be anywhere from $50 or less per month to over $1,000 a month. A recent survey of concierge medical practices found that nearly two-thirds of all concierge medical practices charge less than $180 per month, and a quarter have fees of less than $100 per month, making them very affordable options for individuals and families.

In exchange, the patient has essentially unlimited 24/7 access to the doctor for their medical needs, including regular checkups, treatment for illnesses and injuries, consultations and questions by phone or e-mail, help managing health conditions, referrals to specialists, and even house calls. If you need to go to the emergency room or an urgent care clinic, often your concierge physician will meet you there.

One of the primary benefits of concierge practices is that the doctor typically limits the number of patients in their practice, meaning there is hardly ever a wait to see the doctor. Most patients can be seen the same day, often within an hour or two of calling to schedule an appointment, and because of the limited number of patients, doctors are able to spend more time with each patient and get to know them and their needs better than in a bureaucratic medical practice, where doctors typically only spend a few minutes with each patient before they have to go see the next, often seeing fifty or sixty patients in one day!

One thing to keep in mind is that concierge physicians typically do take insurance, and the retainer fee is on top of whatever services are paid for by the insurer, so you're paying for better access to care, not necessarily a complete escape from bureaucratic medicine.

There are an estimated 3,500 concierge medical practices in the United States, and that number is expected to grow in the coming years.

Similar to concierge practices but generally offering somewhat less access to a doctor is a direct-care practice. Monthly fees are low, often between $50 and $90 a month per person, less for children. While some do provide round-the-clock access similar to a concierge practice, more offer a set number of appointments and services per year or a very low copay per visit.

Epiphany Health, a direct-care practice in Florida, offers members 25 visits a year plus an annual wellness exam, and services provided in their office such as splinting, sutures, nebulizers, abscess drainage, skin biopsies, and joint injections are done at no charge. The large number of primary care visits included in the membership fee ($83 for an individual, plus $69 for a spouse and $49 for a dependent child) are ideal for individuals who have chronic conditions that need regular treatment or examinations, or otherwise make regular visits to a primary care physician.

For the uninsured or those with high-deductible plans, membership in a concierge or direct-care practice can not only provide for almost all their primary care needs at less than the cost of Obamacare insurance but also provides much better access to care and even a higher quality of care because the doctor has fewer patients and more time to spend with you. As an added bonus, there's no government or insurance bureaucrat looking over their shoulder telling them how to practice medicine in an efficient (i.e., cheap) way!

Finding a Concierge or Direct-Care Practice

Here are several online sources for finding one of the thousands of concierge or direct-care practices near you:

- American Academy of Private Physicians, www.privatephysicians.com/##

- Concierge Medicine News, https://secure.jotformpro.com/form/30135370702947

- Direct Primary Care, www.dpcare.org/practices

- MDVIP, www.mdvip.com/

- Concierge Choice Physicians, www.choice.md/locations

- Qliance (Washington, plans to expand to other states), http://qliance.com/

- Medlion (CA, NV, FL, PA, AZ, WA), http://medlion.com/

Convenient Care Clinics

Another great option for self-pay patients is so-called convenient care clinics. These are healthcare clinics typically staffed by nurse practitioners or physician assistants and located in retail locations such as shopping centers, drugstores, and big-box retailers like Target.

These clinics offer affordable care that is typically fairly easy to access and does not require an advance appointment. While they are not able to provide the same scope of services as a physician's office can, they are able to diagnose, treat, and prescribe medications for a wide range of relatively common and uncomplicated illnesses and injuries including strep throat, burns, cuts, pinkeye, ear infections, sprains, and poison ivy, and administer vaccinations as well. They are often open on weekends and outside of normal work hours.

Nurse practitioners typically have a four-year nursing degree and a three-year master's degree, while physician assistants have a four-year undergraduate degree plus two or three years of graduate-level study in medicine. While less experienced and educated compared to a medical doctor, the quality of medicine they practice is generally high, and they know to refer patients to a physician if a patient has an injury or illness that is beyond their ability to either diagnose or treat.

The costs of visiting a convenient care clinic are generally lower than visiting a physician that takes insurance. Minute Clinic, the largest chain of convenient care clinics in the nation and typically found in CVS pharmacies, lists prices of $79 to $89 for most services, including treating sprains, suture and staple removal, urinary tract infections, chicken pox, and monitoring and evaluating high blood pressure, diabetes, and high cholesterol. Because they post their prices, it is relatively easy to know how much your visit will cost, unlike most physicians' offices that are not either cash-only or cash-friendly.

Convenient care clinics typically are able to provide your primary care physician with the records of your treatment as well. They do accept insurance and are often included in provider networks, which can be important for people with high-deductible plans.

The widespread availability of convenient care clinics (there are more than 1,400 clinics across the country, mostly in urban and suburban areas), combined with their transparent pricing and quick accessibility, make them an excellent option for self-pay patients.

Finding a Convenient Care Clinic near You

Convenient care clinics are available in thirty-six states plus the District of Columbia, primarily in easily-accessible retail locations including CVS pharmacies, Target stores, and shopping malls. The links below will allow you to find one near you (some are only in one or a handful of states).

- Healthcare 311 (national finder), www.healthcare311.com

- Minute Clinic (CVS, nationwide), www.minuteclinic.com/

- Take Care Clinic (Walgreens, 18 states), www.takecarehealth.com/Locations.aspx

- ShopKo Fastcare (upper Midwest, Great Plains, West), www.careworkshealth.com/cwh/about_us/locations.html

- Target Clinic (Target, Florida, Illinois, Maryland, Minnesota, North Carolina and Virginia), www.target.com/store-locator/find-clinic

- The Little Clinic (Arizona, Colorado, Georgia, Kentucky, Ohio, Tennessee), www.thelittleclinic.com/Dot_Storelocation.asp?category=118

- Aurora Quickcare Clinics (Wisconsin only), www.aurora-healthcare.org/services/quickcare/index.asp

- Careworks (Pennsylvania), www.careworkshealth.com/cwh/about_us/locations.html

- RediClinic (Texas), www.rediclinic.com/

In addition to the sites listed here, select Walmart stores also have convenient care clinics, typically operated by local providers.

Urgent Care Clinics

Depending on whether you opt for a cash-only, cash-friendly, concierge, or direct-care physician as your primary care provider, or rely on convenient care clinics, you may find yourself in a situation where you need medical care outside of regular hours or that is beyond their scope of practice or skill level.

In many instances emergency care may be the right choice. But getting treatment in an emergency room can be expensive, especially for self-pay patients. In many cases, seeking treatment at an urgent care clinic can be a better choice. More than a quarter of all visits to emergency rooms are unnecessary and could be treated at an urgent care clinic or in a physician's office.

The website for the Urgent Care Association of America describes urgent care clinics this way:

- Urgent care centers provide walk-in, extended hour access to adults and children for acute illness and injury care. Visit an urgent care when your condition is beyond the scope or availability of your regular primary care provider—or not severe enough to warrant a trip to the emergency room.

- Centers are typically staffed with physicians, and may also have physician assistants, nurses, nurse practitioners, medical assistants, and radiology technicians working with patients. Most centers also treat fractures, can provide IV fluids, and have x-ray and lab processing onsite.

- Urgent care centers typically operate 7 days a week (including holidays) and are open between 8 and 9 a.m., and close between 7 and 9 p.m. on the weekdays. Hours may be somewhat earlier on the weekends.

Other injuries and illnesses often treated at urgent care clinics include cuts requiring sutures, allergies, flu symptoms, bronchitis, and falls.

When You Need the Emergency Room

One urgent care clinic posted the following on their website as a guide for when patients should seek care in an emergency room:

Those experiencing a life-threatening illness or injury—such as major head trauma, chest pain, severe abdominal pain, or loss of consciousness—should go directly to an emergency room (ER). The following situations provide a useful guide for understanding what requires ER treatment:

- *Falls from greater than 7 feet*
- *Loss of consciousness*
- *Infants less than 6 months of age or with a temperature greater than 103°*
- *Pregnancy bleeding or complications*
- *Life-threatening allergic reactions*
- *Severe burns*
- *Severe choking (cannot breathe or talk)*
- *Severe abdominal pain*
- *Signs or symptoms of stroke or heart attack*
- *Amputation of a body part*
- *Near drowning*
- *Electrical shock*
- *Open or angulated fractures*

Urgent care clinics also typically recommend that infants and toddlers be treated either by their primary care physician or at emergency rooms.

The savings from going to an urgent care clinic instead of a hospital emergency room can be substantial. One review of the differences between urgent care clinics and emergency rooms looked at the most common illnesses and injuries treated in each setting. Treating acute bronchitis in the ER costs $595 on average, compared to only $127 at an urgent care clinic. Sinusitis costs $617 to treat in an ER, but only $112 at an urgent care clinic. In general, treatment at an ER was between 3 to 6 times more expensive than in an urgent care clinic.

In addition, many urgent care clinics offer discounts for self-pay patients. Healthworks Medical Group, a chain of 200 urgent care clinics in 17 states, promotes its "low-cost, self-pay option for Urgent Care visits" on its website, while Physicians Urgent Care, with 20 locations in 4 states, gives a 30 percent discount to their patients who pay cash.

Concentra, the largest chain of urgent care clinics in the nation with more than 330 clinics in 40 states, posts its prices for self-pay patients. What it terms a basic visit costs between $130 and $170, while an advanced visit costs between $240 and $280. They also offer coupons on their website, as do some other urgent care clinics.

For self-pay patients, going to an urgent care clinic can be a prudent way to save money while still getting the immediate care you need.

Finding an Urgent Care Clinic

There are more than 9,000 urgent care clinics across the nation, located in urban, suburban, and rural areas. Many of them are operated by national chains, others operate clinics in only one or a few states, and some only have a single location. Many are operated by local hospitals as well. The links below should allow you to find one or more urgent care clinics near you.

- Urgent Care Association of America (national trade association), www.urgentcarecenter.org/findacenter.php

- Find Urgent Care(national finder), www.findurgentcare.com/

- Urgent Care Guru (national finder), https://urgentcareguru.com/

- Healthcare 311 (national finder), www.healthcare311.com

- U.S. Healthworks (17 states), www.ushealthworks.com/Services_UrgentCare.html and www.ushealthworks.com/Docs/USH471_CitiesServed2.pdf

- Concentra (40 states), http://maps.concentra.com/corporate/

- Physicians Urgent Care (Illinois, Indiana, Nebraska, Oklahoma), http://physiciansimmediatecare.com/clinics

- MHM Urgent Care (Louisiana), www.mhmurgentcare.com/locations/

- MedExpress (9 states, primarily East Coast), www.medexpress.com/local-centers.aspx

- NextCare (Arizona, Colorado, North Carolina, Ohio, Oklahoma, Texas, Virginia), www.nextcare.com/

Consumer Telemedicine

Another low-cost option for primary healthcare is consumer telemedicine, which offers medical consultation and diagnosis over the phone or by e-mail directly to patients that call or e-mail the service. While it has its limits, for many patients this is a convenient and effective way to handle relatively simple healthcare needs and can be used to avoid more costly visits to a doctor's office.

There are several companies that offer medical services over the phone and through e-mail. Each operate in basically the same way. After signing up and providing medical history information to create an electronic health record that is available for future consultations , patients are able to call in twenty-four hours a day, seven days a week and speak with a practicing physician, or communicate via e-mail.

Doctors are able to advise, diagnose, and even prescribe medications for many basic healthcare needs. Some common ailments that can be addressed through telemedicine include allergies, cold and flu, pink eye, urinary tract infection, rashes, ear infections, and other simple medical issues. They will also advise patients to seek an in-person appointment with their primary care physician or to go to an urgent care clinic or even the emergency room if necessary.

Costs can vary but generally are significantly less than visiting a doctor or convenient care clinic. CallMD offers a family plan for about $200 a year, giving unlimited access to doctors over the phone. Another service, Consult a Doctor, reports an estimated cost of $35 per call. Savings can be substantial when compared to the cost of a visit to a doctor or convenient care clinic, with companies reporting average savings for patients between 10 and 25 percent in healthcare costs.

Some of the consumer telemedicine companies also provide additional benefits (usually for an additional fee), including finding specialists and negotiating for reduced fees, health coaching, and savings on prescription drugs, lab tests, and other healthcare services.

Find a Consumer Telemedicine Provider

The companies below offer patients the ability to consult with a physician by telephone or e-mail for relatively simple ailments and get a diagnosis, treatment recommendation, and a prescription if appropriate. Unfortunately some of the websites are difficult to navigate and find basic information, such as costs.

- 1st Care MD, www.1stcallmd.com/
- Teladoc, www.teladoc.com/
- Ameridoc, www.ameridoc.com/index.html
- Consult a Doctor, www.consultadr.com/index.php
- CallMD, http://callmd.com/offer
- DocDial, www.docdial.com

Medical Discount Cards

One of the perverse outcomes of bureaucratic medicine is that uninsured self-pay patients wind up paying the highest prices for healthcare. This is because large insurers create networks of physicians that agree to give them discounts in exchange for steering large numbers of patients to them. Many doctors have broken out of this system by becoming cash-only or cash-friendly, but many more are still stuck in bureaucratic medicine and if you see one of them, you're likely to be stuck with a higher bill.

There is a solution to this, one that might be particularly attractive for people who have trouble finding a cash-only or cash-friendly practice in their area. Providers of medical discount cards essentially buy access to the discounted rates for their members, allowing patients to pay the reduced prices that insurance companies pay. Most sellers of medical discount cards are independent businesses that buy their access to discounted prices through insurance companies, although some insurance companies including Assurant and a few Blue Cross / Blue Shield companies also sell medical discount cards.

Most medical discount plans include a wide range of health providers, including primary care physicians, specialists, hospitals, pharmacy benefits, dental, and vision care. Some plans are limited to pharmacy, dental, vision, and chiropractic providers.

The savings can be substantial for the uninsured (people with high-deductible plans already have access to the discounted prices and don't need medical discount cards), often ranging between 20 and 40 percent depending on the provider and services. While prices and plans vary from company to company, medical discount cards typically involve a monthly payment of $25 or more.

People considering using a medical discount plan should be aware that the industry has had a problem with poor quality and fraud from some companies. Typical problems include providers not accepting the plans, out-of-date information, deceptive marketing practices that confuse people into thinking they are buying insurance, and fly-by-night scams in which people buy worthless plans.

To combat fraud and stave off regulation that would severely limit the availability of honest discount plan providers, the Consumer Health Alliance (CHA) was created as a trade association for the industry to establish best practices. Among other efforts, they work with regulators and state attorney generals to prevent consumer fraud.

If you are interested in a medical discount card, it's probably a good idea to review and follow the consumer guide provided by the CHA (reprinted nearby) to protect yourself from fraud. You may also want to check with your state's Better Business Bureau, the attorney general's website, or consumer protection agencies to see if any companies you are considering have a history of deceptive practices or fraudulent behavior.

Medical Discount Plan Providers

The following companies provide medical discount plans that give members access to the reduced rates that insurance companies pay healthcare providers. All of them are either members of the Consumer Health Alliance or are insurance companies that sell access to their own network of providers.

- Careington, www1.careington.com/index.aspx
- Coverdell, www.coverdell.com
- DentalPlans.com, www.DentalPlans.com
- New Benefits, www.newbenefits.com
- Aegon Direct Marketing Services, www.aegondms.com
- Alliance HealthCard, www.alliancehealthcard.com
- Brighter, www.brighter.com
- Optum HealthAllies, www.healthallies.com
- Qualbe Marketing Group, www.1dental.com/
- VantageAmerica Solutions, www.VantageAmericaSolutions.com
- Assurant Health, www.assuranthealth.com/corp/ah/HealthPlans/PDMSavingsPlan.htm

In addition, you can check the Blue Cross / Blue Shield company that operates in your area; some of them offer medical discount plans as well.

9 Tips for Shopping for a Discount Healthcare Program

1. Shop around. Every program is different. Find the program that offers the benefits and services that best suit your needs at a reasonable price.

2. Make sure the discount program has clear and under-standable disclosure materials that specifically define the terms and conditions of the program.

3. Look for programs that provide toll-free numbers and/or websites where you can obtain additional information about the programs' benefits and the healthcare providers who are participating in them.

4. Read the program's complaint and refund policies carefully to determine if they are reasonable. The company should offer a 30-day refund policy for your membership fee.

5. Make sure the program's materials clearly state that the discount program is not insurance.

6. Be sure the program's benefits do not duplicate your current healthcare insurance policy or other health benefits offered by your employer.

7. Be wary of any program that requires large, up-front fees.

8. Read all materials carefully.

9. When in doubt about a discount healthcare program, check the company out with your local Better Business Bureau, state insurance department, or state attorney general's office.

Source: Consumer Health Alliance

Online Booking, Shopping, and Bidding

One of the more recent developments benefiting self-pay patients has been the creation of websites geared toward matching them with providers that offer cash prices, provide information on what prices are being paid to providers in an area, and even allow patients to bid out their medical care and get prices below what insurance companies pay. Two of the sites, Medibid and Health Care Blue Book, are particularly valuable for patients seeking hospital-based or surgical care, discussed in the next chapter.

The following are brief descriptions of several websites that you can use as a self-pay patient. Please note that in the fast-moving online world, by the time you read this there may be new companies offering similar or even better services than those described here, or some sites may have gone out of business or changed their model.

- Medibid (www.medibid.com) allows patients to submit the medical procedure or treatment they are seeking, which is then distributed to providers across the country who bid on providing the specified care at a fixed cash price. Patients can accept any of the offers, which include not only price but information about the provider offering the treatment. Patients are under no obligation to select any of the providers who bid on their treatment.

  This provides two benefits: the patient knows ahead of time just how much their care is going to cost, and the prices are typically much lower than list prices that the uninsured self-pay patients might otherwise pay. According to the site, employers who use the service for their employee plans generally save between 25 and 40 percent, and discounts can be up to 80 percent.

A wide range of medical treatments, providers, and facilities are included in Medibid, including overseas providers and facilities. Hospital and surgical services are also available through MediBid. Patients can submit medical treatment requests ranging from a simple annual exam to a full hip- or knee-replacement surgery.

Medibid charges about $25 for a single treatment request, or approximately $5 a month to subscribe to the site.

- Health in Reach (www.healthinreach.com) allows patients to submit through an online portal the medical procedure or treatment they are seeking, although the providers tend to be mostly dental, vision, chiropractic, cosmetic surgery, and other medical services that are not primary, specialty, or hospital care. Discounts off of list prices for healthcare range from 20 to 80 percent. Unlike Medibid, providers in the Health in Reach system do not bid on specific patients; instead, they simply list their prices and provide an easy mechanism to book an appointment. Information about providers is included along with the price.

  The principal benefit provided by Health in Reach is price transparency: patients know exactly how much, in advance, their visit will cost them. Once a patient finds a provider offering the best value, they are able to use the Health in Reach website to book their appointment online. There are no fees to join or use the service.

- MDSave(www.mdsave.com) works similar to Health in Reach, except that like Medibid it offers primary care providers and some specialists as well. Providers list their fees for MDSave members alongside average prices. The site boasts that savings up to 60 percent are available by purchasing them through the site, although individual patients will have different levels of savings.

- Health Care Blue Book (www.healthcarebluebook.com) bills itself as a "free guide to fair healthcare pricing." Modeled after the *Kelly Blue Book*, which gives consumers helpful information when buying or selling automobiles, the Health Care Blue Book (HCBB) gathers information from large databases across the country as well as directly from patients to determine what a fair price for a service is.

  For example, according HCBB, the fair price for a level 2 (minor problem requiring counseling and treatment, may require coordination of care with other providers-approximately 20 minutes with doctor) new patient visit to a doctor's office nationally is $119. The site allows you to get custom data for your own ZIP code. A level 2 visit in Alexandria, Virginia, costs on average $145, while in Des Moines, Iowa, the same visit costs $111.

  One of the features at HCBB is a printed agreement specifying what the fair price is that patients can take to their provider and ask them to give them that price.

  One drawback of the HCBB is that it generates its fair prices largely based on what health insurers pay providers. This means that the prices given can actually be higher than those offered by cash-only or cash-friendly primary care practices, but in areas where cash-friendly options are limited, HBB can be a great starting point for negotiating with providers for a better price (and the site does include a guide to negotiating prices with doctors and hospitals, available at www.healthcarebluebook.com/page_ContactDoctor.aspx).

Chapter 4

Hospitals and Surgery Centers

Finding primary care medical providers that understand the unique needs and circumstances of self-pay patients can be a modest challenge, but as the previous chapter demonstrated, there are a wide range of easily accessible and affordable options that nearly anybody can take advantage of.

Unfortunately it's a bigger challenge for major medical treatments, such as major surgery, overnight stays in the hospital, trips to the emergency room, or treatment for cancer and other serious illnesses. But there are options, and having access to cash-friendly specialists, hospitals, and surgical centers is especially important because while paying inflated list prices for primary care can be infuriating, paying the list price for hospital care can be financially devastating.

A February 2013 article in *Time* magazine exposed to the public one of the dirty little secrets of bureaucratic medicine: uninsured, self-pay patients are absolutely gouged by hospitals in comparison to what insurers and government programs pay. Hospitals have pricelists known as a chargemaster, and the prices of everything from a Tylenol to open-heart surgery are routinely anywhere from three times to one hundred times what insurers and the government might actually pay. On average, according to one report, uninsured and self-pay patients paid three times what insured patients did for the same services.

It is crucial that self-pay patients know their options for avoiding this type of gouging by hospitals. Here are a few ways to get the treatment you need at a reasonable cost.

Cash-Friendly Facilities

Just as there are cash-friendly primary care practices, there are a few hospitals and surgical facilities that give self-pay patients prices that are on par with those insurance companies pay, and even better rates in some cases.

The Surgery Center of Oklahoma is one of a small number of facilities in the country that offer transparent pricing for a wide range of surgical procedures. Like many surgery centers, it is owned by physicians and focuses on a specific area of medical care. Because they are specialized, they often are able to offer higher quality care than general hospitals, particularly in regards to minimizing infections acquired by patients in the hospital.

The prices offered at the Surgery Center of Oklahoma include $3,740 for arthroscopic knee surgery, $2,750 for carpal tunnel release, $3,050 for a tonsillectomy, and $6,990 for an anterior cruciate ligament repair. These prices are all inclusive, meaning they cover the facility cost, the surgeon's and anesthesiologist's fees, and all other costs associated with the procedures performed, including the initial consultation and follow-up care.

These prices compare very favorably to what insurers pay. According to the Health Care Blue Book, the national average for arthroscopic knee surgery is $3,550, and an anterior cruciate ligament repair is $8,250. According to one interview with the center's medical director, their prices are generally 85 to 90 percent less than local hospital's chargemaster prices.

Other surgical centers offer cash-friendly pricing as well, such as Daytime Outpatient Surgical Center in the Dallas/Fort Worth region. As an example of their pricing, rotator cuff repair costs $6,140, better than the national average of $6,663, and undoubtedly much less than the 'chargemaster' price offered by local hospitals.

Cash-friendly policies at general hospitals can also be found. Good Shepard Medical Center in Longview, Texas, lists several cash prices on their site, such as $3,000 for a childbirth delivered via C-section. Because these are hospital prices, they do not include the surgeon's or doctor's fee (but do include the anesthesiologist). The comparable national fee for a C-section would be $6,734 according to the Health Care Blue Book (not including doctor's fee).

Finding a Cash-Friendly Hospital or Surgical Center

Unlike finding a cash-friendly primary care physician or specialist, finding a hospital that lists their prices for specific procedures up front can be a significant challenge. Some hospitals that offer real, up-front prices include

- Surgery Center of Oklahoma, www.surgerycenterok.com/pricing.php, (405) 475-0678

- Daytime Outpatient Surgical Center (Dallas, TX), www.sworthopedic.com/, 817-738-3390

- Good Shepard Medical Center (Longview, TX), www.gsmc.org/, (903) 315-2000

- Thyroid Surgery Center of Texas, http://thyroidcancer.com/, (512) 608-9595

- Oklahoma Heart Hospital, www.okheart.com/cost-packages, (855) 628-6790 or International@okheart.com

- Henry Ford Hospital (Detroit, MI), www.henryfordhospital.com/body_hfh.cfm?id=46244, (800) 436-7936

- Tucson Medical Center, www.tmcaz.com/, (520) 324-5976

There is also a new website that will help self-pay patients compare prices between surgery centers called Surgery Center Network, available at www.surgerycenternetwork.com/.

Medical Tourism/Bidding

While finding hospitals that post their prices for self-pay patients can be difficult, there is another option: medical tourism. A variant of this is bidding out your medical needs to facilities throughout the country or the world.

Medical tourism means traveling to receive your hospital treatment. Many Americans are familiar with the fact that tens of thousands of Canadians come to the United States each year to receive medical treatment that they either cannot get or must endure long waits for back home. The option to travel to another state or even another country is available to U.S. patients as well.

One company that helps to facilitate domestic medical tourism is North American Surgery, which has negotiated cash prices with hospitals and surgical centers in nine states across the country: Arizona, Idaho, Indiana, Maine, Maryland, Montana, Nevada, Oklahoma, and South Dakota. Aside from the South, hospitals in every region of the country are part of North American Surgery's network.

The types of surgeries available at North American Surgery's network of hospitals cover the full range of procedures, including cardiac, orthopedic, and neurological surgery. Many of the facilities they work with are physician-owned specialty hospitals, which can often deliver a higher quality of care than general hospitals.

The process for patients is fairly simple. They provide North American Surgery with information about the treatment they are seeking, after which they receive several options for hospitals that could perform the surgery. After picking a facility, an initial cost estimate is provided. After a consultation with the surgeon the final price is set and payment made, and the surgery is scheduled and performed.

According to North American Surgery's website, the cost of

surgery at their network of hospitals is typically 50 percent less than what insurers pay hospitals.

Another innovative company that helps match self-pay patients with cash-friendly hospitals and surgical centers is MediBid (also described in the previous chapter). Patients register at their site, and then describe the type of medical procedure or service they need (primary care as well as hospital and surgical care). Physicians and facilities that can provide the requested treatments are identified by MediBid, and you are given a list of potential providers that you can then submit your information to asking them to bid on your healthcare needs.

Patients can then review the bids they receive, which include not just the price but also information about the doctor or facility that submitted bids. This gives patients the opportunity to shop for quality as well as price. They can then accept whichever bid they want, or reject all of them. If they accept a bid they get contact information about the doctor or facility and proceed to make their initial appointment and begin the treatment process.

Similar to North American Surgery, patients using Medibid can generally pay about half of what insurance companies pay for the same treatment.

For some, overseas medical tourism may be an option. Travelling to a foreign country may not appeal to everyone, but for the cost-conscious self-pay patient, some of the best deals on hospital care can be found overseas. This option may be especially appealing to patients who originally come from another country with hospitals that provide real prices to self-pay patients, particularly those that still have family in their native country.

According to some accounts, patients can usually save between 50 percent and 90 percent off the cost of a procedure performed in another country compared to the United States. In addition, foreign hospitals that cater to medical tourists typically provide all-inclusive up-front pricing for self-pay patients.

For example, in India a company called Narayana Health offers coronary bypass surgery for about $1,600, compared to an average in the United States of close to $75,000 according to Healthcarebluebook.com.

Frequent destinations for medical tourists heading out of the country include Mexico, India, Spain, Brazil, Philippines, Thailand, Argentina, Panama, Chile, and Singapore.

Finding the Right Hospital or Surgical Center for Medical Tourists

Medical tourism a growing business, and there are several companies and trade associations that can assist patients in finding the right facility that will work with them as a cash-paying patient. Below are several companies that can help, many of them specifically cater to medical tourists traveling overseas but several also provide options in the U.S.

- North American Surgery, http://northamericansurgery.com/, (866) 496-2764
- MediBid, www.medibid.com/, (888) 855-6334 or info@medibid.com
- Health Globe, http://myhealthglobe.com/, (800) 290-0197
- Medical Tourism Association, www.medicaltourismassociation.com/en/index.html
- 360 Global Health, www.360globalhealth.com/, (877) 477-6757
- Best Medical Care Abroad, http://bestmedicalcareabroad.com/, (800) 625-8997
- All Medical Tourism, www.allmedicaltourism.com/

- Health Traveler, www.health-traveler.com/
- Globe Medical Tourism, www.globe-medical-tourism.com/, (888) 976-8966
- Medical Tour Experts, www.mte101.com/, (866) 206.4174
- Medical Tourism Corporation, www.medicaltourismco.com/, (800) 661-2126
- Medvoy, www.medvoy.com/, (866) 245.2069
- Surgical Trip, www.surgicaltrip.com/, (888) 896-3996 or info@surgicaltrip.com
- Medical Tourism, www.medicaltourism.com
- Planet Hospital, www.planethospital.com/, (800) 243-0172

Discounts/Negotiating for Self-Pay Patients

If you can't find a nearby hospital with posted prices and aren't interested in traveling out-of-state or even out-of-country for serious medical care, there is still a more direct option available to self-pay patients needing to be treated in a hospital or surgical center: asking your local facility for a discount.

In recent years, as the phenomenon of hospitals charging outlandish prices to uninsured patients has come to the attention of the media, more and more hospitals are recognizing the need to give a fair and reasonable price to patients who are paying for their own care.

While not as helpful as posting prices, many hospitals have begun to offer substantial discounts off of their chargemaster prices. El Camino Hospital in Silicon Valley, says that they offer an automatic 75 percent off of their bill for patients who pay in full at the time of service (which should give you some idea of how badly they inflate their prices to begin with). Baylor Health Systems, with several hospitals in Texas, offers a 35 percent discount to uninsured patients. Both offer written estimates for the cost of many procedures, although the price is not binding and may be higher or lower in the end.

In some cases, your doctor may be able to help you negotiate a cash price for your treatment at a local hospital. You can also call the hospital billing department directly and explain that you are a self-pay patient and ask how much a particular procedure will cost to have performed at their facility (remember, this probably won't include the surgeon's or treating doctor's fee).

Having a rough idea of what the hospital typically charges insurance companies for similar treatment can be extremely helpful in these circumstances. The Health Care Blue Book, described in the previous chapter, can be a good source for this information.

There are also companies that will help you negotiate your hospital bills, typically for a percentage of the amount saved (this is helpful if you've already received treatment at a hospital). In addition, if you are a member of Christian healthcare ministry, they offer members assistance in negotiating reduced medical bills.

Negotiating a Better Price for Hospital Treatment

The following companies and guides can help you to negotiate better prices for care in a hospital than what cash-paying patients are typically charged:

- My Medical Negotiator,
  www.mymedicalnegotiator.com/

- Medical Cost Advocate, www.medicalcostadvocate.com/
  Default.aspx, (201) 891-8989

- Medical Billing Advocates of America,
  www.billadvocates.com/, (540) 904-5872,
  mbaa@billadvocates.com

- Medical Bill Mediation,
  http://medicalbillmediation.com/, (877) 261-3791

- Hospital Bill Review, www.hospitalbillreview.com/, (800) 906-8085, info@hospitalbillreview.com

- "How To Negotiate a Large Medical Bill" (article), www.changehealthcare.com/downloads/fieldguides/ FGCH001%20Negotiate%20Large%20Bill.pdf

- "How to Negotiate Your Medical Bill," www.webmd.com/ health-insurance/features/negotiate-medical-bill

Seeking the Medically Appropriate Level of Care

Part of being a smart self-pay patient is knowing what level of treatment to seek. How do you know whether you should be going to a retail clinic, a primary care physician, an urgent care clinic, or the emergency room? The following table, courtesy of the Urgent Care Center, may be helpful.

Know your treatment options: You have more than you think!				
Illness/Injury	Retail Health Clinic	Doctor's Office	Urgent Care Center	Emergency Department
Major Illness or Injury (broken bones, burns, bleeding)				X
Chest Pains, Shortness of Breath, and Other Symptoms of Heart Attack or Stroke				X
Significant, Uncontrolled Bleeding				X
No Pulse				X
Spinal Cord or Back Injury				X
Labor				X
Poisoning				X
Minor Fracture			X	X
Animal Bites			X	X
X-rays			X	X
Stitches			X	X
Back Pain		X	X	X
Sprains and Strains		X	X	X
Nausea, Vomiting, Diarrhea		X	X	X
Mild Asthma		X	X	X
Minor Headaches		X	X	X
Foreign Object in Eye or Nose		X	X	X
Blood Work		X	X	X
Allergies		X	X	X
Bumps, Cuts, and Scrapes	X	X	X	X
Rashes and Minor Burns	X	X	X	X
Fevers	X	X	X	X
Burning with Urination	X	X	X	X
Ear or Sinus Pain	X	X	X	X
Eye Irritation, Swelling, Pain	X	X	X	X
Vaccinations	X	X	X	X
Minor Allergic Reaction	X	X	X	X
Coughs and Sore Throat	X	X	X	X
Cold or Flue Symptoms	X	X	X	X
This chart does not contain an exclusive list of illnesses and injuries and should not be considered to be medical advice. If in doubt always err on the side of caution				
Source: http://www.urgentcarecenter.org/about.html				

Chapter 5

Prescription Drugs

Obtaining the prescription drugs you need as a self-pay patient can be just as much a challenge as finding primary care providers and hospitals that are tailored to serving your needs. But just as in those areas, there are a number of options available to both those without health insurance as well as people with high-deductible plans. The following sections describe some of these options.

Cash-Only and Cash-Friendly Pharmacies

Pharmacies are generally run the same way most physicians' offices and hospitals are: set up to deal with insured patients who get a negotiated rate that is often far below the list price. This can often mean self-pay patients having to pay far more for the medications they need than insurance companies and insured patients do and that it can be difficult to even find out what the price of a drug is.

But just as there are doctors that have set up their practices to serve the health needs of self-pay patients, some pharmacies have done this too. Although not nearly as common as cash-only or cash-friendly primary care providers, they do exist and can be a source of big savings. Just as physicians' offices can cut costs by avoiding the costs of dealing with insurance companies, so can pharmacies. They also typically focus on generic drugs, which represent big savings over brand-name drugs.

One such pharmacy is the Rxtra Care Pharmacy chain in the Seattle area. With three locations, they note on their website that "[b] ecause insurance companies do not offer adequate reimbursement for most pharmacy services, including filling standard prescriptions, many companies will increase the cash price of drugs in order to compensate for their losses elsewhere. Our business model is to provide the lowest prices for drugs to cash-paying customers because we don't deal with any insurance companies. We can beat almost any price out there, including Costco."

One additional benefit of cash-only pharmacies is that they often provide additional services including compounding, which means customizing prescription drugs for individual patients' unique needs. This might include converting a drug normally delivered in tablet form to a liquid or adding flavor to a children's drug.

Finding a Cash-Only or Cash-Friendly Pharmacy

Finding a pharmacy that is set up to treat cash-paying patients fairly can be a challenge. There are no associations or lists of cash-friendly pharmacies, but a Google search using the term cash only pharmacy and your local area can help you find any near you. Below are several cash-only pharmacies:

- Rxtra Care Pharmacy (Seattle area, 3 locations), www.rxtracare.net/index.html, pharmacy@rxtracare.net
- MedSave Discount Pharmacy (Minnesota, 2 locations), (763) 252-0094 (Minneapolis) and (218) 720-5850 (Duluth)
- Bill's Pills (Grand Rapids, MI), www.billspillsonline.com/, Bill@BillsPillsOnline.com, (616) 233-9126
- Adam's Discount Pharmacy (Glenside/Philadelphia, PA), http://adamsdiscountpharmacy.com/, (215) 572-1118
- Patient's Choice Discount Pharmacy (Newport News, VA), www.patientschoicerx.com/, (757)283-5882
- MedSavers Pharmacy (Austin, TX), www.medsaversrx.com/, (512) 465.9292

In addition to these and a few other cash-only pharmacies you might find by searching online, you may want to consider two other sources to find pharmacies that are equipped to handle cash-paying patients fairly. Compounding pharmacies are frequently set up to cater to self-pay patients, and you can go to this website to find one near you: www.ecompoundingpharmacy.com/.

Likewise, independent pharmacies can sometimes be a good option for cash-paying patients because the owner and the pharmacist behind the counter are frequently the same person, and they may be more able to deal with customers who do not have insurance. The National Community Pharmacists Association offers an online tool for finding independent pharmacies near you at www.ncpanet.org/index.php/find-an-independent-pharmacy.

Generic Drugs a Great Way to Save Money

When a new drug is developed by a pharmaceutical company, they receive a patent that allows them the exclusive right to make that drug. Because they are the only one making the drug, they are able to charge a high enough price to pay for the research and development costs needed to create the new drug in the first place, typically hundreds of millions or even billions of dollars.

After a drug has been on the market for a number of years (usually anywhere from 6 to 10 years), the patent expires, and then generic drug manufacturers can produce the same drug. Because they don't have to invest nearly the same amount in research and development to make the drug, the price of generics are much cheaper than the original. According to the Food and Drug Administration, generics' average cost is about 80 to 85 percent less than their name-brand competitors.

For example, Lipitor, a popular drug used to treat high cholesterol, is available in both brand-name and generic form. The price at one major pharmacy for 30 tablets of brand-name Lipitor in the 10 mg dose was $137, compared to only $16 for the generic version.

Depending on your doctor, they may write you a prescription for a brand-name medicine. Be sure to ask your doctor if there is a generic drug available that will work just as well. Occasionally patients have specific issues that make the more expensive brand-name medicine the better choice, but usually a generic drug will work just as well while saving you a lot of money.

Chain and Big-Box Pharmacies

While small, independent, cash-only pharmacies as well as compounding and independent pharmacies described earlier often focus on dispensing generic drugs, big chain pharmacies like CVS and Walgreens as well as those located in big-box stores like

Walmart, Costco, and Target can also offer significant savings as well for patients buying generic drugs.

Starting in 2006, Walmart launched a program offering hundreds of different generic drugs at only $4 for a 30-day supply and $10 for a 90-day supply. The generic drugs offered include commonly prescribed medications covering a wide range of illnesses and conditions including asthma, cholesterol, diabetes, high blood pressure, mental health, and thyroid conditions, as well as antibiotics.

Since Walmart launched its $4 generic drugs program in 2006, several other major drugstore chains and big-box pharmacies have followed suit.

The savings can be significant, even for insured patients. A June 2012 article in the *Huffington Post* reported on an Alameda, California, man and his savings at Costco:

> *Morris Pineda of Alameda, Calif., says that learning it was cheaper for him to pay out-of-pocket for his prescription medications instead of putting in a claim with his insurance company came as a "slap in the face."*
>
> *Pineda ... actually didn't believe it when his doctor advised him to fill his seven prescriptions at Costco and "don't tell them you have insurance." Heck, he pays $330 a month for that insurance and he's entitled to some reimbursement for a covered expense, he thought. But by ignoring the coverage he pays for, his drugs now cost him less than $100 a year instead of the $420 his insurance charged in copays for the seven generic drugs.*

For the self-pay patient, purchasing generic medicines at a cash-only, compounding, independent, chain, or big-box pharmacy can be a major source of savings, lowering drug bills by hundreds of dollars a month.

Deals on Generic Drugs at Chain and Big-Box Stores

The following websites for chain and big-box pharmacies list the generic drugs they have available as well as the details of their generic drug program. Some of them require enrollment in the specific pharmacy's program.

- Walmart, www.walmart.com/cp/ PI-4-Prescriptions/1078664

- Target, www.target.com/pharmacy/generics

- Kroger, www.kroger.com/pharmacy/generics/Pages/ default.aspx

- Fred Meyer, www.fredmeyer.com/generic/Pages/default. aspx

- HyVee, www.hy-vee.com/health/pharmacy/generics/ default.aspx

- CVS, www.cvs.com/promo/promoLandingTemplate.jsp?pr omoLandingId=healthsavingspass

- Walgreens, www.walgreens.com/images/psc/pdf/VPG_ List_Update_03-21-2013.pdf

- Rite Aid, www.riteaid.com/phar- macy/prescription-savings/ rite-aid-prescription-savings-program

- Costco, www2.costco.com/Pharmacy/DrugInformation. aspx

Shopping Around

Prices charged from one pharmacy to another can vary significantly. Often pharmacies will sell a handful of drugs at rock-bottom prices in the hope that patients will buy their other, more expensive (compared to what other pharmacies are charging) drugs while buying their "bargain-priced" drug. Shopping around and comparing prices on all your drugs can result in big savings if you can find the lowest-price drug available at different pharmacies.

There are websites and even apps for smart phones that will allow you to compare drug prices at different pharmacies. The site www.WeRx.org and their mobile app provides price information on hundreds of different drugs around the country, making comparison shopping fairly easy. Other sites and apps give similar information for both brand and generic drugs.

Online & Mobile Tools for Pharmaceutical Shopping

The following sites allow prescription drug shoppers to compare prices in their local area and find the best deals:

- GoodRx, www.goodrx.com/
- WeRx, http://werx.org/
- Rx Price Quotes, www.rxpricequotes.com/
- LowRx, http://lowrxcard.com/

WeRx and GoodRx both offer mobile apps as well. Lowest Med, https://new.lowestmed.com/, and LowRx, http://lowrxcard.com/, also offer apps you can download that allow you to compare prescription drug prices on your smartphone. In addition, some of these sites and apps offer coupons from drug manufacturers that can be used to reduce prices even further.

Discount Cards

As with most elements of bureaucratic medicine, self-pay patients buying prescriptions can be stuck with the list price for medications, which can be much higher than what insurance companies and insured patients pay. Fortunately, cash patients can also get the lower negotiated price for prescription drugs by purchasing a drug discount card or joining a drugstore's discount club.

Several of the chain and big-box pharmacies listed above offer pharmaceutical discount programs for self-pay patients, and many of the companies listed in chapter 3 in the *Medical Discount Card* section offer discounts on pharmaceutical drugs as well. Some of these cards and programs are free, while others require a one-time or monthly fee.

Pharmacy Discount Cards

Below are several companies and organizations that offer discount programs for prescription drugs, in addition to many of those listed in this chapter's section Chain and Big Box Pharmacies as well as some in chapter 3's section Medical Discount Cards. Many of them are free.

- NeedyMeds, www.needymeds.org/
- The Healthcare Alliance, http://thehealthcarealliance.com/
- Your Rx Card, www.yourrxcard.com/
- Familywize, http://familywize.org/
- Coast to Coast Rx Card, http://coast2coastrx.com/
- Together Rx Access, www.togetherrxaccess.com/

Other Options for Cutting Drug Costs

Here are a few additional suggestions on how to cut your prescription drug costs:

1. Buy a 90-day supply. Typically, buying your drugs for a 2- or 3-month period can result in savings. Mail-order pharmacies are often your best option for extended supplies.

2. Split your pills. Many drugs (not all—consult your pharmacist) can be split in half with an inexpensive pill cutter. If your prescription calls for you to take 10-milligram pills, you can sometimes get 20-milligram pills for just a little more than the lower dose, effectively cutting your cost in half!

3. Get samples from your doctor. Pharmaceutical companies frequently give free samples of new drugs to doctors. If your doctor recommends a brand-name drug and discourages you from using a generic, ask if they have any free samples.

4. Use coupons. Many drug manufacturers offer coupons on their websites that can lower the costs of prescription medicines.

5. Consider whether you really need a prescription drug at all. For some simple illnesses, like a cold or the flu, over-the-counter medicine can be almost as effective and significantly less expensive.

Drug Assistance Programs

Going to a cash-only or cash-friendly pharmacy, using generic drugs whenever possible, and shopping for the best deals can save the self-pay patient hundreds of dollars each month. But that may not be enough for some drugs, especially for newer medicines including those that treat serious illnesses and conditions like cancer, AIDS,

Crohn's disease, and many other ailments. Many of these drugs can cost thousands or even tens of thousands of dollars a month!

Fortunately there are a variety of options for uninsured patients or those who need assistance because of high deductibles or their insurance doesn't cover certain treatments. Many drug companies offer free or reduced-price drugs to patients who can't afford needed medicines. There are also state-run and privately run programs that can help get free or reduced-price drugs for patients.

The pharmaceutical industry sponsors a program called the Partnership for Prescription Assistance that connects patients with nearly two hundred pharmaceutical companies as well as hundreds of state-run and private programs. In addition, some disease-specific advocacy groups, such as the American Cancer Society and the American Diabetes Association, also have information online about pharmaceutical assistance programs, and there are even organizations that directly assist patients by helping to pay their drug costs.

These programs are aimed at helping uninsured patients. Self-pay patients who are members of healthcare-sharing ministries or who received a lump-sum payment from a critical illness policy are still eligible for these programs, although some may also have hardship, income, or asset tests that may make some people ineligible.

Accessing Pharmacy Assistance Programs for the Uninsured/ Self-Pay Patient

There are several sources online that can help you to find free or reduced-price prescription medicines. In addition, your doctor may be able to assist you.

- Partnership for Prescription Assistance, www.pparx.org/, (888) 477-2669

- Rx Assist, www.rxassist.org/, info@rxassist.org

- Rx Outreach, www.rxoutreach.com/, (800) 769-3880

- Together Rx Access, www.togetherrxaccess.com/, (800) 444-4106

- State Pharmaceutical Assistance Programs, www.medicare.gov/pharmaceutical-assistance-program/ state-programs.aspx

- Needy Meds, www.needymeds.org/index.htm, (800) 503-6897

- Prescription Assistance Program, http://prescriptionassistanceprogram.com/index.php, (573) 996-3333, Info@PrescriptionAssistanceProgram.com

- Rx Hope, www.rxhope.com/, (877) 267-0517, CustomerService@RxHope.com

- Patient Assistance Link, www.patientassistancelink.org/

Chapter 6

Imaging, Screening, Labs

One of the most critical elements of modern medicine is the ability to use high-tech imaging (like CAT scans and MRIs), screening, and laboratory testing to identify serious injuries and illnesses, as well as assess the risks that individuals have for specific illnesses like cancer. These technologies can allow for better treatment and help people to reduce their chances of getting ill.

The good news for self-pay patients is that, unlike most of the rest of bureaucratic medicine, many of these technologies are relatively easily accessible and at reasonable prices that don't gouge self-pay patients. In some cases, the screenings and tests are available for free through companies and community or health groups.

X-Rays, Ultrasounds, MRIs, and Other Imaging Services

Having an MRI, ultrasound, or other imaging service that can provide your doctor with an inside look at your body is a common part of healthcare today. While some doctors (and nearly all hospitals) have imaging equipment like X-ray machines in their office, there are many standalone imaging centers that can often provide the same services at a much lower cost. Because they are independent firms that are accustomed to dealing with self-pay patients (particularly those with high deductibles), they often have fair, transparent prices.

Because prices for MRIs and other imaging services can vary widely depending on the provider (hospitals often have wildly inflated chargemaster prices for imaging services), it is recommended that you use the Health Care Blue Book (described in chapter 3) to get a rough idea of what a fair price is in your area, and compare prices between different providers.

Where to find MRIs, Ultrasounds, and Other Imaging Services

The following sites can help you to find a place to get your imaging services done. Most imaging requires a referral from a doctor, who can probably also recommend local facilities.

- MRINet, www.mrinet.net/
- Medtronic, www.medtronic.com/mrisurescan-us/mri-centers.html
- American College of Radiology, www.acr.org/Quality-Safety/Accreditation/Accredited-Facility-Search
- Save On Medical, www.saveonmedical.com/

Lab Testing

Another key element of modern medicine is laboratory testing, typically of blood, urine, or skin tissue. These tests can reveal conditions and illnesses that doctors can't see or confirm in an office visit, as well as providing important monitoring of chronic conditions that are being managed. Among the things that labs test for are allergies, cancer, heart health, cholesterol, diabetes, infectious diseases, kidney and liver diseases, thyroid conditions, and vitamin deficiencies.

While hospitals can provide laboratory services, their prices reflect bureaucratic medicine and often charge the highest prices to uninsured or self-pay patients. Fortunately there are several national chains offering laboratory testing at prices that can be 80 percent or more below what hospitals charge.

One such company is First Choice Labs USA, which promotes itself as offering "discount lab services at competitive pricing." According to one article about the company, an insured patient (!) who was charged $414 for her share of the cost of lab tests at another facility would have only paid $95 for the same tests with First Choice Labs USA. They offer facilities across the country where you can give your blood, tissue, or other specimen, as do other national chains.

In addition to the companies identified below, your doctor may be able to recommend local labs that also provide low-cost laboratory services for self-pay patients.

Finding Lab Services at a Fair Price

- First Choice Labs USA, http://firstchoicelabsusa.com/
- Laboratory Corporation of America, www.labcorp.com
- Quest Diagnostics, www.questdiagnostics.com/home/patient-home.html
- MD Lab Tests, http://gads.mdlabtests.com/
- Save On Labs, www.saveonlabs.com/default.asp
- EconoLabs, www.econolabs.com/
- True Health Labs, www.truehealthlabs.com

Getting Screened for Illness and Risks

Screenings for various illnesses, which can determine not only whether you have a specific illness but also whether, based on your specific health status and family history, you are at an increased risk of developing an illness in the future, can be an important part of your healthcare. Some of the illnesses that can be detected or assessed for risk through screenings include cancer, diabetes, high blood pressure, heart disease, and several others. Early detection of disease or learning early on that you face a high risk of getting a disease can lead to improved health and reduced medical bills.

There are numerous companies that will conduct comprehensive screening for illnesses and risk of illness. Because insurance companies often don't cover screenings for diseases, the industry has had to develop prices, packages, and services for self-pay customers.

One company that has an innovative, customer-centric focus is HealthFair, which has a mobile screening facility in a bus that travels the country. They offer transparent pricing, such as a basic package including screenings for heart disease, stroke, and aneurysm that costs $179.

Whether you need to undergo screening is an individual choice, one that perhaps your doctor can help with. While many people find value and comfort in getting screened even if they don't have any symptoms or known risk factors for any diseases, others might consider it a waste of money. For those who do want to get screened, businesses that do the screening are accustomed to dealing with self-pay customers.

> ### Screening for Health
>
> Below are several suggestions for finding a firm that will conduct routine and advanced screening on your health status and risk of developing many common diseases.
>
> - Healthfair, www.healthfair.com/
> - Life Line Screening, www.lifelinescreening.com/default.aspx
> - Princeton Longevity Center, www.theplc.net/

In addition to paying for screenings, which can be more convenient, many businesses, health facilities, and private organizations frequently sponsor free screenings for a wide array of diseases and conditions, and there are probably several near you.

One company offering free screenings is CVS, which through its Project Health provides free testing for high blood pressure, obesity, bone density, diabetes, and high cholesterol. Sam's Club members can also receive free screenings, which are grouped around a specific theme each month. For example, in August 2013, Sam's Club offered a Children's Health and Back to School free screening package that included blood pressure, Body Mass Index, and vision screenings, while their October Women's Health free screening package included tests for blood pressure, body mass index, thyroid, a take-home gel breast self-exam kit, and sight.

Medical facilities and organizations also offer free screenings to the public, frequently sending their health professionals into the community with special vehicles or by attending health fairs. Baptist Health System in San Antonio, Texas, offers testing and screening for cholesterol, blood pressure, obesity, and risk assessments for heart disease, stroke, and diabetes. New York Presbyterian Hospital offers free cancer screenings monthly for uninsured residents in the New York metropolitan area.

Many communities hold health fairs that offer free screenings, sometimes organized by private groups and sometimes put on by public health officials. An April 2013 event in Los Angeles offered free screenings for cholesterol, asthma, allergies, diabetes, dental problems, high blood pressure, and other health problems, while an event in Portland, Oregon, that same month offered free screenings for diabetes, vision problems, glaucoma, and high blood pressure.

Disease-specific nonprofit groups often sponsor or promote free screenings as well, including the American Kidney Fund. A nonprofit organization focused on kidney diseases, they offer free health screenings around the country and in a wide variety of venues including churches, health fairs, businesses, colleges, and community centers. In 2013 they will hold more than a dozen free kidney screenings around the country in Atlanta, Chicago, Houston, Jacksonville, Washington DC, and other cities.

Screenings for disease, which can diagnose or assess a patient's risk of getting ill, can be valuable. Early detection can lead to early treatment, which is typically far less expensive and more effective than late detection. Likewise, learning that you are at high risk for specific diseases can help lead to lifestyle changes that can dramatically lower your chances of needing expensive medical care in the future while improving your health.

Where to Find Free Screenings

The list below only scratches the surface of where you can find free screenings for a wide variety of illnesses and conditions. In addition to the recommendations below, you should check your local public health department's website, which will typically list local health fairs that offer free screenings.

- Kidney Fund, www.kidneyfund.org/get-tested/

- National Breast and Cervical Cancer Early Detection Program, http://apps.nccd.cdc.gov/dcpc_Programs/default.aspx?NPID=1

- American Society for Dermatological Surgery, www.asds.net/find_volunteer.aspx

- ZERO (prostate cancer), http://zerocancer.org/events/free-testing/

- Prostate Conditions Education Council, www.prostateconditions.org/screening-site

In addition, local and state chapters of the American Cancer Society frequently have information about free or reduced-cost cancer screenings, you can find information on your local area at www.cancer.org/myacs/index, and searching online with the terms free, health, and screening along with your city or region can also help find additional options.

Chapter 7

Vision and Oral Care

Although they often get less attention than high-priced care delivered in hospitals or routine primary care provided in a medical doctor's office, vision and oral care can be crucial as well. Several years ago the *Washington Post* reported the sad tale of a young child who was in and out of the bureaucratic medical system, sometimes covered by Medicaid and sometimes not. Because of difficulty finding a dentist who would take Medicaid, the boy didn't have a decayed tooth removed. Eventually it developed into an infection that killed him.

Fortunately, oral and vision care have only recently begun to be absorbed by bureaucratic medicine, meaning that many providers still are able to provide real and transparent prices for most routine services, including dental checkups, eye exams, teeth cleaning, and other treatments. Countless stores offer eye exams, and big-box retailers like Walmart and Target usually have eye clinics on their premises.

This means that, unlike other chapters in this book, there is little need for additional information for how to find a self-pay friendly provider of oral or dental care. Pretty much anybody you find in your community is going to be well accustomed to dealing with patients who pay for their own care. It still pays to call and compare prices, though, and if you hear of a dentist or optometrist that doesn't accept insurance, that's probably your best bet.

For more expensive treatments and services, which can be thousands of dollars, dentists are often accustomed to working out payment plans. In addition, many of the discount cards for health services cover dental treatments.

One additional option to consider for dental treatments is low-cost care provided by clinics at dental schools. These clinics give dental students an opportunity to practice their skills, and they are closely supervised by the professional dentists on staff at the schools. You can find a list of dental schools across the country at the website of the American Dental Association, www.ada.org/267.aspx.

Chapter 8

Mental Health

M ental health covers a wide variety of conditions and treatment options. Sometimes depression is a temporary issue, related to a recent painful or upsetting event like job loss or romantic breakup and requiring relatively modest mental health services. In other instances depression can be a long-term and severely debilitating condition requiring ongoing counseling and support as well as expensive medications. On the severe end, it can lead to inpatient confinement.

Because of this, the situation for self-pay patients seeking any sort of mental health treatment is mixed. Patients with moderate needs can probably get the services they need by relying on a cash-friendly doctor or therapist, as discussed in chapter 3.

Because many prescription drugs used to treat mental illnesses and conditions are also available in generic form, the advice in chapter 5 will be helpful. For example, a 100-day supply of the generic form of Prozac, used to treat depression, is available at Costco for less than $10, compared to nearly $750 for the brand-name medication at the same store.

There are also numerous alternatives that can cost less or even be free that may be appropriate for those with relatively modest mental treatment needs. Many religious pastors are able to provide counseling for common issues, and schools that offer masters- or doctorate-level degrees in counseling, psychology, and related fields often have free clinics. Free hotlines can also be used, such as that operated by National Suicide Prevention Lifeline.

For more serious issues, good options can be limited. Organizations like Alcoholics Anonymous or Narcotics Anonymous can be helpful to those dealing with substance abuse issues, as can religiously-oriented programs like TEEN Challenge, which features nearly two hundred residential treatment centers throughout the country.

In addition, many mental health professionals offer what is called a sliding scale of fees, meaning they are willing to reduce their rates to accommodate patients for whom paying the full rate would be a hardship and even offer free services to some patients.

While staying out of the bureaucratic medical system may be important for some, there may be times when treatment services offered by the state are the only option. In the event of an involuntary commitment to a psychiatric facility, a court order by a judge is typically required. Among other options for state-provided mental health treatments, you may need to consider a community health center that offers mental health services or a public hospital that offers inpatient psychiatric treatment. You can find information on these through the U.S. Department of Health and Human Services' Substance Abuse and Mental Health Services Administration or the local affiliates of the National Alliance on Mental Illness, among other sources.

Another critical source of information on mental health treatment options is your own primary care or mental health professional, who can take your self-pay status into account when making recommendations.

Mental Health Options for Self-Pay patients

Unlike previous chapters, there are no readily identifiable one-stop online sites that can be used by self-pay patients to find the best, most cost-effective ways to save money while getting their mental health needs met. But the agencies, organizations, and sites below can be helpful in navigating this vital area of healthcare. Remember that that information in chapters 3 and 5 can be helpful as well as your own doctor and mental health professional.

- Suicide Prevention Hotline, www.suicidepreventionlifeline.org/, (800) 273-8255

- Substance Abuse & Mental Health Services Administration, http://findtreatment.samhsa.gov/, (800) 662-4357

- TEEN Challenge USA, http://teenchallengeusa.com/

- National Alliance on Mental IIlness, www.nami.org/Template.cfm?Section=Your_Local_NAMI&Template=/CustomSource/AffiliateFinder.cfm

- Mental Health Alliance, www.mentalhealthamerica.net/go/searchMHA

- National Parent Helpline, (855) 427-2736

- Alcoholics Anonymous, www.aa.org/

- Narcotics Anonymous, www.na.org/

- National Association of Community Health Centers, www.nachc.com/findahealthcenter.cfm

Chapter 9

Public and Private Charity Care

Even after trying some or even all of the options described in previous chapters, your financial situation or healthcare needs may be so dire that you have to seek charity care in order to pay your medical bills, or even public assistance through Medicaid or some other program.

Every situation is unique, but here are a few things to consider if you find yourself in this position:

1. Nonprofit hospitals, which are more than half of all hospitals in the country, are required by their tax status to provide charity care. Obamacare strengthens this requirement, partly in response to several scandals in the last decade in which nonprofit hospitals were sending bill collectors after uninsured patients unable to pay inflated medical bills. While Obamacare does not specify how nonprofit hospitals are to deliver charity care or decide who may be eligible for free or reduced-price care, it does require that they have written guidelines and policies on these matters that are available to the public. If you need medical treatment at a hospital that can be scheduled in

advance, you may want to contact their charitable care coordinator to discuss receiving free or low-cost treatment.

2. Hospitals are required to provide medically necessary care to patients who arrive in their emergency room without regard to whether they are insured or not. The downside is that even though they have to treat you, they can bill you the inflated chargemaster rates if you don't qualify for their charity care program. Medical billing negotiators (see chapter 4) can help negotiate down these rates after the fact if need be. The important thing to remember is that in the event of a medical emergency, you can get the care you need.

3. There are more than 1,200 free and charitable clinics across the country that can deliver high-quality primary care as well as mental health, oral, and vision services to the uninsured and indigent. They are staffed by volunteer medical professionals from the local community and rely almost exclusively on private donations for funding. The hours can be limited, but they offer an option for care that fills a need for many. While free clinics typically focus on primary care, they can also refer patients to specialists and hospitals for free or reduced-price care, as well as provide free prescription drugs. You can find one of these clinics near you at the website of the National Association of Free and Charitable Clinics, http://nafcclinics.org/. You can also find Christian clinics focused on delivering care to the poor through the Christian Community Health Fellowship at www.cchf. org/.

4. For decades, the federal government has supported thousands of community health centers across the country. Like the free clinics, they focus on providing free or

reduced-price primary care based on a patients' ability to pay and can also provide care for mental health and substance abuse problems as well as dental care and prescription drugs. Doctors and other medical professionals at these facilities are typically paid staff. You can find a directory on the website of the U.S. Department of Health & Human Services at http://findahealthcenter.hrsa.gov/Search_HCC.aspx.

5. A majority of doctors still provide some charity care in their own practices. They understandably have to limit the number of free or reduced-price patients they see, but if you already have a relationship with a doctor they may be willing to provide charity care if you explain your financial situation.

6. There are several charities that assist patients with paying medical bills. The Cancer*Care* Copayment Assistance Foundation helps to pay medical expenses related to cancer, with grants typically being in the $2,500 to $5,000 range. The Healthwell Foundation provides similar support for patients facing a wide range of treatment needs, giving approximately $124 million in 2011 to more than 44,000 patients. Others that offer similar assistance can be found through online searches.

7. Several children's hospitals that provide care regardless of a family's ability to pay exist around the country. The most famous of these is probably St. Jude Children's Research Hospital in Nashville, Tennessee, which treats catastrophic illnesses in children, primarily cancer. The Shriners have also set up several hospitals around the country in twenty U.S. cities, including Boston, Chicago, Houston, Los Angeles, Salt Lake City, Shreveport, and Tampa. Like St.

Jude, they treat regardless of a family's ability to pay, with a focus on orthopedics, burns, and spinal cord injury.

8. Individuals with significant medical expenses are able to raise money from friends, family, acquaintances, and strangers. There are several websites online help to raise funds for medical care, including www.giveforward.com/, www.gofundme.com/, www.youcaring.com/, https://fundrazr.com/, www.indiegogo.com/, and www.donationto.com/.

These options described aren't the only ones for patients with significant medical needs who are facing serious financial difficulties, but they describe some of the more widely accessible ones. Simply searching online using terms like *charity medical care* can provide additional options.

And finally, Obamacare can be a safety net. Depending on the severity and timing of your healthcare needs and financial situation, what previously might have been considered an unaffordable health insurance policy might seem a bargain in the face of major medical expenses.

Chapter 10

Options for Employers

For most Americans, healthcare has been tied to employment beginning with the wage and price controls imposed by the federal government during World War II. This in many ways created the bureaucratic medical system we have today, which Obamacare largely builds on.

As a result, many employers feel obligated to offer health benefits in order to attract and retain employees or feel it's their responsibility to provide this important benefit. It may even be a good investment in your business because healthy employees may be more productive, take less sick time, and generally contribute to employee satisfaction. In addition, Obamacare requires businesses with more than fifty full-time employees to offer health coverage to their employees or face fines.

But for many employers who want to offer health coverage to employees, the costs can be prohibitive, and the quality of benefits can suffer because all they're doing is signing up for the bureaucratic medical system . Fortunately employers have many options for providing health benefits while avoiding bureaucratic medicine.

Unlike the options discussed in previous chapters of this book for being a self-pay patient, setting up employee health benefits that largely operate outside of the bureaucratic medical system requires professional advice, usually from a benefits consultant or insurance broker. The following information briefly describes several options that a consultant or broker should be brought in to help determine if they are appropriate for your business.

Understanding Obamacare for Employers

Before looking at options, it is important to understand exactly how Obamacare affects businesses.

The good news is that small employers, defined as those with fewer than 50 full-time employees (or the equivalent) are exempt from Obamacare's mandate to offer health insurance. There are tax subsidies for businesses with fewer than 25 employees who do offer coverage, but most businesses seem to be ignoring them because they are quite modest for all but the smallest employers, aren't available to businesses that pay their employees more than $50,000 annually on average, can only be taken for two years, and are complex and difficult to apply for.

If a small employer does decide to offer health insurance, it must offer the expensive insurance required under Obamacare, and it may have to pay a minimum percentage of the premiums depending on the state it resides in.

For large employers, defined as having 50 or more full-time employees, Obamacare can be much more onerous, although it also may offer more flexibility in some ways. Large employers are required to offer health insurance to all full-time employees or else pay a $2,000 penalty for each employee (although no penalty is assessed on the first 30 employees, so a company with exactly 50 full-time employees that doesn't offer health insurance would pay a $40,000 penalty (50 – 30 = 20, × $2,000 = $40,000).

In addition, a large employer offering health insurance that is deemed unaffordable (would cost an employee more than 9.5

percent of their income for an individual policy) or doesn't offer the minimum benefits mandated by Obamacare would have to pay a $3,000 penalty for each employee that chooses instead to buy a policy on an Obamacare exchange and receives a tax credit for their coverage.

Beyond that, large employers do have some options and flexibility. They can self-insure, which will be less expensive for companies that have younger, healthier employees on average. They only have to offer insurance to full-time employees (those working thirty hours or more per week), so they can avoid the cost of providing health insurance by reducing hours for some employees below the threshold. They can experiment with innovative plan designs that don't meet Obamacare's mandates, hoping they save more money with the plan than the penalties they might be assessed if a few employees opt for coverage through an Obamacare exchange and receive tax credits. Finally, depending on the cost, it may actually be cheaper to drop coverage entirely and pay the fine if it is less than what the company would otherwise pay in health premiums.

The following sections describe some specific options for employers both large and small who prefer to stay out of the bureaucratic medical system but still want to provide some level of healthcare benefits to employees. Many of these options can be combined, potentially offering a generous benefit for employees while avoiding the bureaucratic medical system and saving money for both employee and employer. As noted before, each of these should be examined in full with a professional benefits consultant or insurance broker.

One innovative benefits specialist in this area is Ralph Weber of Route Three Benefit Consultants in Tennessee (Ralph is also the creator of the Medibid.com website discussed in chapters 3 and 4). He has developed an approach that allows companies to maximize their employee benefits while minimizing any tax penalties. Ralph can be reached at rfweber@routethree.com or 888-720-8889.

One additional note: on July 2, 2013, the Obama Administration delayed the requirement that large employers offer coverage or pay a tax. Originally scheduled to go into effect in 2014, the employer mandate will not be implemented until 2015.

Critical Illness, Accident, and Fixed-Benefits Policies

As described in chapter 2, these policies provide lump-sum cash payments to the insured, which can be used to pay for their health-care. Although they don't satisfy the requirement for large employers to provide coverage to employees or pay a fine, they can in fact be tax deductible as compensation for employees just like other benefits.

As noted before, these policies are generally inexpensive compared to health insurance. They are frequently offered by employers today (although not usually as a substitute for health insurance), and insurance brokers are accustomed to dealing with employers who want to offer this benefit to employees. Some insurance companies, in fact, only offer these policies through employers and not through the individual market. You can also determine how much of the premium you want to pay, anywhere from 0 to 100 percent.

Skinny Plans

Before Obamacare, some employers began offering what were known as "mini-med" plans. These plans were aimed at relatively low-wage employees who mainly needed affordable access to primary care. The maximum benefit amount per year was typically $10,000 or less, and employees could buy them for as little as $10 or $15 per paycheck. In return employees had access to routine primary care providers at low or no cost to them.

Now called skinny plans, they appear to satisfy Obamacare's requirement that large employers offer health insurance to all full-time employees, but they don't meet the requirement for adequate coverage with minimum benefits. What this means is that a large employer offering a skinny plan is exempt from the $2,000-per-employee fine but not the $3,000 fine for each employee receiving a tax credit on an Obamacare exchange. The benefit of offering this approach is that while the tax for not offering any insurance is $2,000 per employee after the first 30 employees, the $3,000 penalty is only assessed on those workers who reject the skinny plan and instead opt to buy coverage through the exchange and who receive tax credits.

Because these policies are typically aimed at employers with relatively young and healthy employees, they can still be much less expensive than paying for comprehensive coverage that meets Obamacare's minimum benefit standards. If a 100-employee company offering a 'skinny' plan only had 5 employees receive tax credits on an Obamacare exchange, that $15,000 penalty plus the employer share of the premiums is likely to be far less expensive than paying a $140,000 penalty for not offering any health insurance or several hundred thousand dollars to provide insurance that includes all mandated benefits.

As an alternative to a skinny plan, one that offers a similar type of benefit at a low cost that employers can also pay to enroll employees in is a direct primary care practice, discussed in chapter 3. This may be an ideal option for employers with younger, healthier workforces that mainly need access to primary care.

Self-Insurance

When a company self-insures, it means they don't actually buy insurance on behalf of their employees. Instead they agree to pay directly for their employees' healthcare costs. Companies that self-insure typically hire a benefits manager to manage the health plan (often an insurance company), which usually looks to all the world like any other health insurance plan with employees paying a share of their premiums as well as copays, deductibles, and co-insurance, and offering all the other normal features of health insurance.

The difference is in who is taking the risk of having to pay for higher-than-expected medical costs; in an insured plan the insurance company accepts the risk and will lose money if they underestimate how much medical care a particular company's employees will use during the year, while in a self-insured plan the employer faces the risk of having to pay more than anticipated if employees consume more healthcare than expected.

For this reason, the self-insured option has typically been used only by very large companies with hundreds or even thousands of employees. The reason is simple: a larger employee base helps to spread the risk of a few major catastrophic medical expenses, while a small company can be financially devastated by a single cancer patient with tens or hundreds of thousands of dollars in treatment expenses.

Self-insurance can be appealing to small businesses that have younger or healthier employees than average because the total healthcare expenses are likely to be lower than what they might have to pay for insurance purchased through an Obamacare exchange, but concern about a single employee racking up huge medical bills can understandably scare small businesses away from this option.

New offerings by some insurance companies can put the self-insurance option back on the table for small employers. Called stop-loss insurance, it protects small businesses from bearing the risk of a single employee driving them out of business with unexpected medical expenses. It allows small businesses to buy insurance that will limit how much they might have to pay in the event of large and unexpected medical expenses.

The way it works is fairly straightforward. An employer might expect that their fifteen employees plus their dependents will have total medical expenses for the year of $100,000, which is less than the $150,000 in insurance premiums they might otherwise pay would be. If the business would normally split the premiums 50/50 with their workers, the employer would save $25,000 by becoming self-insured, savings which can be used to invest in the business, raise wages, or be taken as profit, and the employees also save $25,000 in premiums that they don't have to pay.

But what happens if instead of medical expenses being $100,000 for the year, they unexpectedly rise to $400,000 after one employee is diagnosed with cancer and another gets into a serious car accident? With a stop-loss policy set at $150,000, the employer only has to come up with an additional $50,000 ($150,000 stop-loss limit, minus $100,000 initially set aside by the employer and collected from employees as premiums) to pay the bills, which is far better than having to come up with an additional $300,000 that would drive most small businesses into bankruptcy.

Self-insured plans also don't need to include all of the benefits that are mandated for health insurance policies sold on Obamacare's exchanges, although if they don't, companies with more than 50 employees can be hit with a $3,000 penalty for each employee who chooses not to buy into the self-funded plan and instead gets a tax credit while purchasing a policy through the individual exchange.

Summary of Employer Options

Many employers, especially smaller businesses or those with primarily low-wage employees, will have some tough choices under

Obamacare. Small businesses that are exempt from the mandate may still need to offer some sort of health benefit in order to attract and retain qualified employees, while larger employers may need to find some option they can pursue that avoids most of the penalties for not offering insurance while still lowering their costs for health benefits.

The options outlined in this chapter may help to "thread the needle" for these businesses. For example, providing enrollment in a direct primary care practice for employees along with fixed-benefit and critical-illness policies is likely to cost only a fraction of what a full Obamacare policy will cost, while providing a similar level of benefits.

Just as important, these options can actually help to improve employees' access to affordable quality medical care by getting them out of the bureaucratic medical system. By working with professional benefits consultant or insurance broker, you can explore your options as an employer and find ways to save money while still providing a health benefit for your employees.

Chapter 11

People like You

Will the options outlined in this book work for most people? Will they work for you? The short answer is probably, but not necessarily.

Nearly all of the alternatives to Obamacare for getting needed healthcare described in this book currently exist and are being used today pretty much exactly as described. Obviously they are not in widespread practice though, and for some people their medical needs are so severe that, as bad as it is, the bureaucratic medical system is their best option today.

To help you understand how the options described in this book might or might not work for you, I've created several fictional people and families to describe how they might fare as self-pay patients. Although these people are fictional, they are based loosely on people I know who are or have been in similar situations and either have or could benefit from the options described below.

Tom, Age 26, Single Male, Generally Healthy, Income $35,000

Tom works as a photographer in a local studio that doesn't offer insurance, and has no known medical issues. Under Obamacare, Tom could buy a high-deductible policy for about $160 a month that would cover most medical expenses after a $6,400 deductible is met. He is not eligible for a subsidy.

As an alternative, for around $20 a month, Tom could buy a critical illness policy that would give him up to $50,000 if he is diagnosed with cancer, has a heart attack, or is afflicted with some other serious condition. For an additional $20, he can get an accident insurance policy that will pay $100 for a trip to the emergency room and $1000 for a night's stay in the hospital, among other benefits.

If Tom chooses to pay the penalty for being uninsured, in 2016 he would pay a $695 penalty. Combined with his $40 a month premiums for the critical illness and accident policies, his out-of-pocket costs are $1,175 for the year, or $745 less than the $1,920 it would have cost him to buy a catastrophic plan.

Now imagine Tom gets diagnosed at age 26 with testicular cancer. Treatment often means surgical removal of the testicles, a procedure that the Health Care Blue Book says costs $5,764 and includes a 2-night hospital stay. Presumably there would have been several hundred or even thousands of dollars worth of doctors' visits and diagnostic tests leading up to the surgery.

If Tom had purchased the catastrophic plan, his total out-of pocket costs including premiums would have been around $8,300. But with his critical illness policy, Tom receives a $50,000 benefit to pay his medical bills plus funds during his recovery time and any follow-up care that may be needed. In addition he will receive $1,250 from his accident insurance policy ($1,000 for the first night's stay in the hospital, $250 for the second night). He has *no* out-of-pocket expense in the end because of the generous payouts.

Kate, Age 33, Single Female, Chronic Digestive Problem, $46,000 Income

Kate works as a fundraiser for a small nonprofit that can't afford to offer health benefits. She has been diagnosed with irritable bowel syndrome and takes medication daily to deal with it but is otherwise in good health and only visits her primary care physician and gynecologist for routine exams. Her income is too high to qualify for subsidies through the exchange, and the cost of insurance would be about $210 a month and it would have a deductible of about $5,000.

As a sufferer of a chronic disease, getting the necessary medications to control her symptoms is high on the list of Kate's priorities. Her doctor prescribed an anti-spasm drug, Bentyl, for her to take four times a day to deal with pain. Buying the brand-name drug would cost her about $42 for 120 tablets at her local pharmacy, which would last her about 1 month. By purchasing the generic at Costco, she can cut that price by nearly 80 percent, paying a little less than $9 for a one-month supply—less than the copays that most insured pay!

For her routine medical needs, including an annual physical and gynecological exam, Kate visits doctors that don't accept insurance or a convenient care clinic, keeping her out-of-pocket costs for doctor's visits to about $300 a year.

In addition, because Kate is concerned about what might happen if she were to get seriously injured or ill, she purchased a short-term health insurance policy that has a deductible of $12,500 and only costs her $40 a month. Even if she winds up paying the Obamacare fine of about $900, Kate is still able to save nearly a thousand dollars a year compared to if she'd bought the Obamacare plan and can sleep at night knowing that in the event of a major medical need she has insurance to cover it.

Judy, Age 27, Single Female, Obese and Pre-Diabetic, $29,000 Income

Judy works as a cook at a small restaurant that doesn't offer health insurance. She is eligible to receive subsidies that will help lower the cost of insurance through an Obamacare exchange, but she would still have to pay about $130 a month for a policy with a $5,000 deductible.

She wants to have bariatric surgery performed, which she and her doctors believe is the best option for her to lose the weight she needs to avoid becoming diabetic. Even under Obamacare, however, bariatric surgery would not be covered by the policy she could purchase, meaning she would have to pay for it out of her own pocket. She is willing to pay out of pocket for the surgery, but is shocked to find the listed price for bariatric surgery in her area is about $23,000.

Judy is also a devout Christian; in fact, her parents were missionaries in Africa for many years, and she has traveled the world with her parents. She can join a healthcare-sharing ministry for about $45 a month that will cover medical expenses above $5,000, equivalent to the Obamacare policy she could have bought for $130 a month. By doing this, she's able to save more than $1,000 a year. In addition, because members of healthcare-sharing ministries are exempt from the mandate to purchase insurance, Judy does not have to pay any penalty tax.

But the healthsharing-ministry won't cover the bariatric surgery either. Fortunately, Judy is able to work with a company specializing in medical tourism and finds a superb hospital in India that will perform the surgery for less than $7,000. Having traveled the world, she is comfortable going overseas for her operation, and friends of her family live in the same city and have offered to let her stay with them before and after the procedure. Knowing how important this is to her future health and that it may be her best chance to avoid diabetes, she is willing to pay for it on her credit card and pay it off over time, including using the money she saved by not purchasing Obamacare insurance to pay it off.

James and Ellie, Ages 37 and 34, Plus 3 Children, Generally Healthy, Income $75,000

James works as a project manager for a homebuilder while Ellie stays home and cares full-time for their children. His employer offers subsidized insurance to James, but adding his wife and children would require them to pay nearly $8,000 a year to be covered through his employer, and they can't afford that much. Because his employer does offer insurance, however, they aren't eligible for any Obamacare subsidies. They decide to decline any insurance from James' employer.

As parents with three young children, they are regularly taking one or more of their children to the doctor for checkups and for minor ailments and injuries. James and Ellie decide to sign up their children for a direct care practice that allows each child 20 visits with a primary care doctor per year, for a total of only $105 a month. They also decide to buy short-term insurance with a high deductible for themselves and each of their children, which costs them another $150 a month to insure against a catastrophic medical expense. In all, their healthcare costs are about $3,000 a year, far less than the $8,000 in premiums they would have had to pay for James' employer plan.

At the time of this writing, it is not clear whether James and Ellie would have to pay the penalty tax for being uninsured. Although the out-of-pocket premiums exceed 8 percent of their income, potentially making them exempt from the mandate, the fact that James's employer offered him alone "affordable" insurance may require him to pay a penalty for not being insured himself. If the maximum possible penalty is applied, James and Ellie would still save almost $3,000 by choosing alternatives to Obamacare.

David and Margaret, Ages 51 and 50, Somewhat Healthy, 2 Children, $110,000 Income

David and Margaret are owners of a small business with no employees. Their two children are physically active teenagers, both of whom play sports. Margaret is healthy other than occasional migraines, while David has high blood pressure, high cholesterol, and some arthritis and tendonitis.

Buying an insurance policy for themselves under Obamacare would cost about $12,000 a year for a policy with a family deductible of $10,000, money that they want to put back into their business so it can grow instead. Because the premium exceeds 8 percent of their income, they are exempt from the mandate to purchase insurance, but with moderate health issues themselves and children that play sports, they feel it's important to have some sort of coverage.

To address their own health issues, they purchase critical illness and fixed-benefit plans that between them will provide funds to pay healthcare expenses in the event of a serious medical event like a heart attack, major surgery, or cancer. Because they are both in their fifties, the policies are more expensive than someone younger might pay, totaling about $400 per month. By purchasing generic and over-the-counter medicines for their own medical conditions and visiting doctors that don't accept insurance, they are able to keep their monthly health bills other than their insurance to about $100.

They also purchase short-term insurance policies for their children, adding another $100 per month to their expenses.

While David and Margaret's total annual health bill still come to nearly $7,000 a year, they are far better off than if they paid the $12,000 a year for Obamacare insurance, especially considering that with an Obamacare plan they'd still need to pay more for their medications and doctor visits and have to pay up to $10,000 on top of their premiums in order to meet the deductible and get much benefit from their Obamacare policy.

Gary and Connie, Both Age 59, Moderately Unhealthy, $59,000 Income

Gary and Connie both work at a medium-sized business that provides a high-deductible ($7,000) insurance plan and matches their contributions to a health savings account. They pay approximately $5,000 a year for their employer-provided policy and have been putting about $2,000 a year into their HSA. Because Gary has chronic heart disease and high cholesterol and Connie suffers from diabetes and high blood pressure, they typically spend all of the HSA funds each year on prescription drugs and doctor's visits.

The most important thing to Gary and Connie is to manage their health spending wisely, stretching every dollar in order to avoid going too far beyond the funds set aside in their HSA each year. Because they both make relatively frequent trips to the doctor to monitor their health and to help manage their chronic conditions, they join a direct primary care practice for $50 each a month.

Gary and Connie between them have 7 prescriptions to help manage and treat their illnesses, 5 of which have generic versions available. Purchasing generics at 90-day supply quantities through a big-box retailer keeps their spending on those drugs to less than $20 a month. For the two more expensive drugs as well as Connie's diabetes testing supplies, they have found a cash-only pharmacy that can provide them with reduced-cost drugs.

By being cautious consumers of healthcare goods and services, comparing drug prices, and paying attention to their own medical needs, Gary and Connie are able to wisely manage their scarce healthcare dollars and know that in the event of a big medical bill, they have the high deductible policy to cover it.

Is Being A Self-Pay Patient Right for You?

The examples described above are fictional (although based loosely on people I know), but they hopefully give you a sense of how the alternatives to Obamacare described in this book might work for you (or how they might not). Each and every person is going to have to decide for themselves whether they can make some combination of the options described here work for them.

If one of the examples above sounds like you, then it might be easy for you to see how one (or more likely several) of the options explained in this book could meet your healthcare needs. If not, here are a few questions you might want to consider as you weigh whether and how to be a self-pay patient:

1. Are you relatively healthy? Generally speaking, a healthy person who expects to continue to be healthy is more likely to benefit from some combination of the options in the book than someone who is relatively sick.

2. Can you afford the cost of an Obamacare insurance policy? The subsidies for purchasing insurance through the exchange are generous to some but fairly small for a large number of people and nonexistent for many more. Can you afford to put nearly 10 percent of your pre-tax income toward health insurance?

3. Will you get value out of an Obamacare insurance policy? Even if you can afford it, it might not make sense to you to pay thousands of dollars each year for a policy that you only get a few hundred dollars' worth of healthcare benefits from.

4. Do you want to have relatively fast access to doctors? Because of the way Obamacare was designed and is being implemented, many who remain in the bureaucratic medical system will have long waits to see a doctor. Those who opt out and become self-pay patients will likely enjoy same-day access to their healthcare providers.

5. Do you want doctors that work for you or for insurance companies and government bureaucrats? Obamacare encourages healthcare practices where the doctor's incentive is to reduce the amount of care they provide in order to save money. It also encourages "cookbook" medicine where many major medical decisions are made based on how average populations respond to treatment, not on your specific and unique needs as determined by your doctor. Self-pay patients, on the other hand, have only their doctor to deal with in deciding what treatments are appropriate.

6. Are you comfortable having your medical records widely available to thousands of employees at insurance companies and the government? Key components of Obamacare involve putting your private medical records into huge databases where anybody with the right access can get at them.

7. Do you have a high-deductible health plan that effectively makes you a self-pay patient for most or all of your healthcare needs? Even if you have insurance, the options and

strategies outlined in this book can help you to stretch your health dollars as far as they will go.

8. Are you able to self-fund your expected healthcare needs with some combination of income, savings, retirement funds, home equity, investments, or other assets?

These are just a few of the many, many questions you should ask yourself when deciding whether to buy an Obamacare insurance policy or set a different course with some combination of the options described in this book.

Chapter 12

Wrapping Up

The focus of this book has been you and your medical needs and how to get the healthcare you need even if you don't have traditional insurance or have a high-deductible plan that requires you to pay for a significant share of your care before insurance begins to pay benefits. Hopefully, you have read this book and found information that will allow you to navigate the healthcare marketplace, get the care you need, and avoid as much as possible the bureaucratic medical system that needlessly inflates costs, invites government and insurance company bureaucrats to interfere with and dictate your care, and in too many cases diminishes the quality of care you receive.

As I said at the beginning, the options described in this book are not suitable for everyone. But they probably are suitable for most people if they are willing to become even modestly engaged patients and healthcare consumers.

Depending on your individual health needs, you may need to spend very little time in preparing yourself to be a self-pay patient. For people who have minor or moderate health needs (which is most of us), the important things to do include:

1. Choose your medical financing arrangement for major

health needs, such as a high-deductible health insurance policy, healthcare-sharing ministry, short-term insurance, self-insurance, or critical illness, fixed benefit, or accident insurance.

2. Find an appropriate medical provider that you can see for your routine healthcare needs, such as a convenient care clinic or cash-only doctor's office.

3. Know where your nearest urgent care clinic is so that in the event of a sudden medical need that doesn't require an emergency room visit you can go to a facility that can treat you without gouging you.

4. If you have children or health needs of your own that require regular treatment, depending on age and their medical needs, consider finding a direct primary care provider that guarantees quick access to a doctor for a reasonable price.

5. If you need to purchase prescription drugs, shop around, and focus on generics if they are available.

For the vast majority of Americans, these five simple things can result in major financial savings, improved access to healthcare, and even a better quality of care. If you or a family member happens to be among the small number of people who have more severe health needs, hopefully this book includes options that will work for you, too.

While this book contains a great deal of information about how self-pay patients can get the healthcare they need even without the sort of comprehensive Obamacare insurance plans that the government wants them to buy, it is hardly complete. Because healthcare providers that cater to self-pay patients operate in a true marketplace, there are always new and innovative companies and organizations entering the marketplace (and some leaving the marketplace as patients find they don't provide enough value for their healthcare dollar).

That means being an engaged patient and healthcare consumer doesn't necessarily end with reading this book and embracing one or a few of the options described here. For updated information about currently existing and new companies that didn't make it into this book, as well as additional resources, check out my blog: www.theselfpaypatient.com. Hopefully, as Obamacare is fully implemented and more people realize that for whatever reason they can't or don't want to be part of the bureaucratic medical system, more innovative providers will enter the market and offer even more options for self-pay patients.

In addition, I highly recommend that you regularly follow the blog of Michelle Katz, author of *Healthcare for Less* and quite accurately described in her Facebook profile as "America's leading source in navigating through the healthcare system while avoiding medical debt." She routinely appears in the media showing how both insured and uninsured people can get the healthcare they need without racking up massive bills. I regularly tell people 'If you're a self-pay patient and you aren't following Michelle Katz, you're doing it wrong.' You can follow her at www.nursemichellekatz.blogspot.com/.

Finally, I've tried to make this book different than most other books on the market about healthcare and Obamacare by ignoring the politics and policy and just focusing on the day-to-day realities and options that Americans with high-deductible insurance or no insurance face in getting the healthcare they need. That said, if you are interested in learning more about public policy alternatives to

Obamacare and the bureaucratic medical system, I strongly recommend you do three things:

1. Read anything ever written on healthcare by John
    Goodman, president of the National Center for Policy
    Analysis. While there is no shortage of great minds writing,
    researching, and speaking about the importance of markets
    in healthcare, John stands above the rest. His recent book
    Priceless was a source for me in writing this book, and he
    closely follows and reports on new and innovative providers
    of healthcare services. You can follow him at http://health-
    blog.ncpa.org/.

2. Subscribe to *Health Care News*, published by The
    Heartland Institute. This monthly public policy newspaper
    covers what is going on in the world of healthcare from
    a free-market perspective and provides excellent coverage
    of what some of the most innovative and groundbreaking
    researchers and analysts are doing and saying. Several of
    the options for self-pay patients written about in this book
    were first written up by me as articles in *Health Care News*
    when I worked at Heartland, including cash-only pharma-
    cies and healthcare-sharing ministries. You can subscribe
    for free at http://heartland.org/subscribe.

3. Join the Association of American Physicians and Surgeons,
    the premier organization in the country for physicians and
    patients interested in healthcare freedom and a true market
    for medical goods and services. By joining you will receive
    regular updates on market-based healthcare reform. You
    can find more at www.aapsonline.org/.

There is a great deal more out there on public policy alternatives to Obamacare and the bureaucratic medical system, but simply doing these three things will introduce you to a much wider discussion and debate being held by a wide range of experts including doctors, academics, think-tank scholars, industry executives, elected officials, and others committed to expanding healthcare access through markets, not mandates.

Finally, please consider letting me know about your own experience as a self-pay patient, for better or worse. I'd love to be able to pass along (while respecting your privacy) to a wider audience how your individual healthcare needs were or weren't able to be met by any of the options described in this book or if you were able to find an even better option that wasn't described here! I can be reached through my blog at www.theselfpaypatient.com.

About the Author

S ean Parnell is a public policy consultant with more than a decade of experience in healthcare, including currently running the website www.TheSelfPayPatient.com and serving as Adjunct Scholar in Health Policy for the Rhode Island Center for Freedom & Prosperity. Other experience includes writing several policy studies on specialty hospitals and the Patient Protection and Affordable Care Act, working for the congressman who was the main author of the Patients' Bill of Rights, and writing for *Health Care News* at The Heartland Institute. Parnell lives in Alexandria, Virginia, with his wife, Anne, and son, Ryan.